Guide to SOC Analyst

Practical Guide

A. De Quattro

Guide to SOC Analyst

Introduction

In today's digital age, businesses and organizations of all sizes rely heavily on information technology systems to operate efficiently. However, with the rapid growth of these systems comes a corresponding increase in cyber threats. The protection of sensitive information and the safeguarding of an organization's digital assets are paramount, especially given the potentially devastating consequences of a data breach. This is where the Security Operations Center (SOC) comes into play.

A SOC serves as the backbone of an organization's cybersecurity strategy. It acts as a centralized unit that manages security across the organization by monitoring, detecting, responding to, and preventing cyber threats. The professionals within a SOC, known as SOC Analysts, play a crucial role in this operation. Their responsibilities span the spectrum of threat intelligence, incident response, and compliance, making them indispensable to an organization's cybersecurity posture.

This text will explore the core elements of a Security Operations Center, the roles and responsibilities of SOC Analysts, and the overarching goals and importance of cybersecurity in safeguarding today's digital world.

Chapter 1: What is a SOC?

A Security Operations Center (SOC) is a dedicated facility where an organization's information systems are monitored and defended against cyber threats on a continuous basis. Think of it as the nerve center of an organization's cybersecurity efforts. A SOC typically operates 24/7 to ensure round-the-clock protection against emerging threats, fueled by the increasing volume and sophistication of cyberattacks.

The SOC is an integral part of an organization's IT security infrastructure, designed to gather, analyze, and act on data concerning potential cybersecurity incidents. By employing advanced technology, a SOC can identify abnormal patterns of behavior within a network, manage threats, and initiate appropriate responses.

Key Functions of a SOC

1. **Monitoring**: The primary function of a SOC is to continuously monitor the organization's IT environment. This involves real-time surveillance of network activity, endpoints, and systems to detect suspicious behaviors or anomalies that could signal a cyber threat.

2. **Incident Response**: Upon detecting a potential cyber threat, the SOC team will initiate an incident response protocol. This includes analysis, containment, eradication, and recovery processes to address the threat and minimize harm to the organization.

3. **Threat Intelligence**: A SOC also plays a vital role in threat intelligence gathering. This involves researching emerging threats, vulnerabilities, and attack vectors to stay ahead of potential attackers. By integrating threat intelligence into their operations, SOC teams can enhance their ability to

preemptively combat cyber threats.

4. **Compliance and Reporting**: Many organizations must adhere to various regulatory standards regarding data protection and security. The SOC is crucial in producing reports and documentation that confirm compliance with these regulations. This also involves conducting regular security audits and assessments.

5. **Collaboration and Communication**: A SOC typically works in conjunction with various other departments within an organization such as IT, legal, and human resources, coordinating efforts to bolster the overall security landscape.

Components of a SOC

To function effectively, a SOC requires various components, which can be classified into:

1. **People**: The talent within the SOC is its most valuable asset. SOC analysts come with diverse skills and expertise levels. The team is typically structured in tiers, with more experienced analysts focusing on complex threats.

2. **Process**: Defined processes and protocols ensure that the SOC operates efficiently and effectively. This includes incident response playbooks, threat-hunting methodologies, and guidelines for reporting and compliance.

3. **Technology**: SOCs employ a range of tools and technologies to support their functions. This can include Security Information and Event Management (SIEM) systems, intrusion detection systems, and endpoints protection solutions.

4. **Data**: A SOC relies heavily on data for its operations. This includes logs, alerts, incidents, and threat intelligence feeds that inform the team's decision-making processes.

The Evolution of SOCs

The landscape of cybersecurity is constantly evolving, and so too are Security Operations Centers. Initially, SOCs were largely reactive, responding to incidents after they occurred. However, in recent years, organizations have shifted towards a more proactive approach, investing in technologies and strategies that enable predictive analytics and enhanced threat detection capabilities. The emergence of Artificial Intelligence (AI) and Machine Learning (ML) in threat detection is also transforming SOC operations, enabling faster and more accurate identification of potential threats.

The Role and Responsibilities of a SOC Analyst

SOC Analysts are the frontline defenders in the battle against cybercrime and play an essential role in the operations of a Security Operations Center. Their responsibilities can vary significantly based on their level of experience, the size of the organization, and the complexity of security needs.

Key Responsibilities of a SOC Analyst

1. **Monitoring and Analysis**: SOC Analysts continuously monitor security alerts generated by security tools. This involves analyzing logs, events, and alerts to identify patterns that may indicate security incidents. Analysts must possess strong analytical skills to discern genuine threats from benign activity.

2. **Incident Triage**: When a potential threat is detected, SOC Analysts are responsible for assessing the severity and likelihood of an incident. This involves prioritizing incidents based on criteria such as impact and urgency, determining whether escalation or further investigation is necessary.

3. **Incident Response**: In the event of a confirmed security incident, SOC Analysts follow established incident response protocols. They collaborate with other teams to contain and mitigate the threat, conduct forensic analysis, and ensure system recovery.

4. **Threat Hunting**: Proactive threat hunting is a critical function of SOC Analysts. This involves searching for hidden threats within the network, employing threat intelligence and analytics to uncover vulnerabilities before they can be exploited by attackers.

5. **Documentation and Reporting**: After handling an incident, SOC Analysts document actions taken and findings in detail. This documentation is critical for regulatory compliance, future incident responses, and organizational learning.

6. **Collaboration and Communication**: SOC Analysts must work collaboratively with other teams, such as Incident Response Teams, IT infrastructure, and executive management. Effective communication ensures a cohesive response to incidents and fosters a culture of security awareness across the organization.

Skills Required for a SOC Analyst

Being an effective SOC Analyst requires a unique skill set that combines technical, analytical, and interpersonal abilities.

1. **Technical Proficiency**: SOC Analysts need a solid understanding of various technologies, including firewalls, SIEM systems, intrusion detection systems, antivirus solutions, and network protocols. Familiarity with scripting and programming languages can also be advantageous.

2. **Analytical Thinking**: The ability to analyze complex data and identify anomalies is crucial. This involves critical thinking and the ability to make sound judgments based on data-driven insights.

3. **Attention to Detail**: Cyber threats can often be subtle and difficult to detect. Analysts must possess keen attention to detail to catch indicators of compromise that may be overlooked by others.

4. **Communication Skills**: Effective

communication is essential for SOC Analysts, as they must convey technical information to non-technical stakeholders. Writing clear and concise reports after incidents is also critical.

5. **Adaptability**: The field of cybersecurity is dynamic and rapidly evolving. SOC Analysts need to be adaptable, willing to learn new technologies, methodologies, and emerging threats.

Goals and Importance of Cybersecurity

Cybersecurity has emerged as a cornerstone of modern organizational strategies, addressing the threats posed by a wide range of attackers. With the increasing digitization of services, the need for robust cybersecurity measures has never been more crucial.

Primary Goals of Cybersecurity

1. **Confidentiality, Integrity, and Availability (CIA)**: These three pillars define the primary goals of any cybersecurity framework. Protecting sensitive information (confidentiality), ensuring that data remains unaltered (integrity), and maintaining access to critical systems (availability) are fundamental objectives.

2. **Risk Management**: Cybersecurity aims to identify, assess, and mitigate risks associated with cyber threats. Organizations implement various strategies to minimize their exposure to vulnerabilities, including conducting risk assessments and adopting layered security controls.

3. **Compliance**: Many organizations are subject to regulatory requirements regarding data protection and privacy. Cybersecurity ensures that organizations adhere to laws and standards such as GDPR, PCI-DSS, and

HIPAA, reducing the risk of legal penalties and reputational damage.

4. **Incident Response**: An effective cybersecurity program includes a well-defined incident response plan. This enables organizations to promptly detect and respond to security breaches, minimizing the impact of incidents on business operations.

5. **Awareness and Education**: Cybersecurity also aims to foster a culture of security awareness within organizations. Employee training and awareness programs are critical components in mitigating risks associated with human error and social engineering attacks.

The Importance of Cybersecurity

1. **Protection of Sensitive Data**: Organizations handle vast amounts of

sensitive information, including customer data, financial records, and intellectual property. Cybersecurity protects this information from unauthorized access and data breaches.

2. **Operational Continuity**: Cyberattacks can result in significant operational disruptions. A robust cybersecurity framework ensures that organizations can maintain continuity in their operations, reducing downtime and associated costs.

3. **Reputation Management**: A data breach can severely damage an organization's reputation, leading to loss of customer trust and potential revenue decline. By prioritizing cybersecurity, organizations can protect their reputation and foster customer confidence.

4. **Financial Security**: The financial implications of cyberattacks can be devastating, with potential losses resulting

from both direct attacks and the costs associated with recovery efforts. Implementing strong cybersecurity measures helps mitigate these financial risks.

5. **Competitive Advantage**: In a world where consumers are increasingly aware of cybersecurity issues, organizations that demonstrate a commitment to security can differentiate themselves in the marketplace. Strong cybersecurity practices can serve as a selling point for customers.

Cybersecurity is no longer an optional consideration but a necessity for the modern organization. The establishment of a Security Operations Center, the critical role of SOC Analysts, and the importance of cybersecurity at large are all essential elements to creating a secure and resilient organizational environment. As technology continues to evolve, so too must the strategies and practices employed to protect against cyber threats.

Chapter 2: Foundations of Cybersecurity

As technology continues to advance at a rapid pace, the importance of cybersecurity has become increasingly critical. The vast array of information and systems at our disposal is constantly at risk of being targeted by various threats. This chapter delves into the foundational concepts of cybersecurity, outlining the basic concepts, the various types of threats and vulnerabilities, the different types of cyber attacks, and the essential practices for risk management and vulnerability analysis.

2.1 Basic Concepts of Security

2.1.1 Definition of Cybersecurity

Cybersecurity refers to the practices, processes, and technologies that are designed to protect computer systems, networks, and data from theft, damage, disruption, or unauthorized access. The ultimate goal of cybersecurity is to ensure the confidentiality, integrity, and availability (CIA triad) of information.

- **Confidentiality** ensures that sensitive information is accessed only by authorized individuals.

- **Integrity** involves maintaining the accuracy and reliability of data by protecting it from unauthorized modifications.

- **Availability** means that information and systems are accessible and usable upon demand by an authorized user.

2.1.2 Key Concepts

In order to grasp the fundamentals of cybersecurity, it is essential to understand several key concepts:

- **Assets**: These encompass anything of value to the organization, including data, hardware, software, and networks.

- **Threats**: Any potential danger that can exploit a vulnerability to cause harm to assets.

- **Vulnerabilities**: Weaknesses or flaws in a system that can be exploited by threats.

- **Countermeasures**: Actions taken to reduce risks associated with threats and vulnerabilities.

2.1.3 Security Policies

Security policies are formal documents that outline how an organization intends to protect its information technology assets. A well-defined policy provides a framework for establishing security measures and sets the expectations for all employees. Key aspects of a security policy include:

- **Acceptable Use Policies (AUPs)**: Guidelines defining acceptable behaviors regarding the use of IT resources.

- **Access Control Policies**: Rules regarding who can access specific data and systems.

- **Incident Response Plans**: Procedures to follow when a security breach occurs.

2.2 Threats and Vulnerabilities

2.2.1 Understanding Threats

The cybersecurity landscape is constantly evolving, with various types of threats emerging every day. Understanding these threats is crucial for organizations to develop effcctive sccurity strategies.

- **Malware**: Malicious software that can infect a computer or network, including viruses, worms, trojan horses, and ransomware.

- **Phishing**: A social engineering tactic that involves tricking individuals into revealing sensitive information like passwords or credit card numbers.

- **Insider Threats**: Security breaches caused by individuals within the organization, either maliciously or unintentionally.

2.2.2 Assessing Vulnerabilities

Vulnerabilities can be classified into several categories, which can help organizations prioritize their security efforts:

- **Software Vulnerabilities**: Flaws in software applications and operating systems that can be exploited.

- **Configuration Vulnerabilities**: Weaknesses resulting from improper configurations of systems and networks.

- **Human Factors**: Mistakes made by

employees, such as using weak passwords or falling for phishing scams.

2.2.3 The Threat Landscape

Cyber threats can originate from various sources, including:

- **Cybercriminals**: Individuals or groups that engage in illegal activities for financial gain.

- **Hacktivists**: Individuals or groups that use hacking as a means of promoting a political agenda.

- **Nation-State Actors**: State-sponsored entities that conduct cyber operations to advance national interests.

2.3 Types of Cyber Attacks

Understanding the various types of cyber

attacks is critical for individuals and organizations to defend against them effectively.

2.3.1 Common Types of Cyber Attacks

- **Denial-of-Service (DoS) Attacks**: Exploiting vulnerabilities in systems to make them unavailable to intended users. Distributed Denial-of-Service (DDoS) attacks use multiple devices to overwhelm a target.

- **SQL Injection**: A technique used to exploit vulnerabilities in web applications by injecting malicious SQL code to manipulate databases.

- **Cross-Site Scripting (XSS)**: An attack that involves injecting malicious scripts into webpages viewed by users.

2.3.2 Advanced Persistent Threats (APTs)

APTs are sophisticated, targeted attacks in which an intruder gains access to a system and remains undetected for an extended period. APTs are typically launched by skilled adversaries, often nation-state actors, with the intent of stealing sensitive data or intellectual property.

2.3.3 Social Engineering Attacks

Social engineering involves manipulating individuals into divulging confidential information. Common tactics include:

- **Pretexting**: Creating a fabricated scenario to obtain information.

- **Baiting**: Offering an enticing incentive to lure individuals into providing information or downloading malicious software.

2.3.4 Ransomware Attacks

Ransomware is a type of malware that encrypts files on a victim's computer, effectively locking them out of their data until a ransom is paid. The increasing prevalence of ransomware attacks highlights the need for strong backup solutions and security measures.

2.4 Risk Management and Vulnerability Analysis

2.4.1 Importance of Risk Management

Risk management is a critical aspect of cybersecurity that involves identifying, assessing, and prioritizing risks followed by coordinated efforts to minimize, monitor, and control the probability of unforeseen events.

2.4.2 Risk Assessment Process

The risk assessment process typically includes the following steps:

1. **Identifying Assets**: Cataloging all assets and their respective importance.

2. **Identifying Threats and Vulnerabilities**: Understanding potential threats that could exploit vulnerabilities.

3. **Assessing Risks**: Evaluating the likelihood and potential impact of identified threats.

4. **Implementing Controls**: Establishing security measures to mitigate risk.

5. **Monitoring and Reviewing**: Continuously tracking and reassessing risks and controls.

2.4.3 Vulnerability Analysis

Vulnerability analysis involves identifying, quantifying, and prioritizing vulnerabilities in a system. Effective vulnerability management requires:

- **Regular Scanning**: Utilizing automated tools to scan systems for known vulnerabilities.

- **Patch Management**: Keeping software and systems up to date with the latest security patches.

- **Penetration Testing**: Simulating attacks to identify weaknesses before they can be exploited by malicious actors.

2.4.4 Developing a Security Framework

A robust security framework integrates risk management and vulnerability analysis into a coherent strategy. Popular frameworks include the NIST Cybersecurity Framework, ISO/IEC 27001, and the CIS Controls. These frameworks provide guidelines for establishing and maintaining a secure IT environment.

The ever-growing threat landscape underscores the importance of a strong foundation in cybersecurity principles. By understanding the basic concepts of security, recognizing threats and vulnerabilities, being aware of various types of cyber attacks, and instituting effective risk management practices, organizations can significantly enhance their ability to protect their information systems and mitigate risks. The digital world may present numerous challenges, but with the right knowledge and tools, individuals and organizations can navigate this complex landscape securely.

Chapter 3: Security Infrastructure

In today's digital world, where cyber threats are evolving at an alarming rate, having a sound security infrastructure is crucial for organizations to protect their sensitive data and maintain operational integrity. This chapter delves into the intricacies of a Security Operations Center (SOC), focusing on its architecture, the tools and technologies employed, and the management of logs and event monitoring. A thorough understanding of these components is essential for establishing a robust security framework that can effectively respond to threats in real time.

3.1 SOC Architecture

The architecture of a Security Operations Center (SOC) serves as the backbone of an organization's cybersecurity efforts. A well-designed SOC architecture is essential to ensure that the security team can efficiently monitor, detect, and respond to security incidents.

3.1.1 Core Components of SOC Architecture

A typical SOC architecture consists of various layers that work together to facilitate effective security monitoring and incident response. These layers include:

- **Data Collection Layer**: This layer involves the acquisition and aggregation of data from various sources within the organization, including endpoints, servers, firewalls, intrusion detection systems (IDS), and more. The data collection is essential for gaining visibility into potential security incidents.

- **Data Processing Layer**: Once data is collected, it moves to the processing layer, where it is normalized, filtered, and enriched with contextual information. This layer is vital for minimizing false positives and ensuring that security analysts focus on significant potential threats.

- **Data Analysis Layer**: At this level, security analysts and automated systems analyze the processed data to identify patterns, anomalies, and threats. This layer often employs advanced algorithms, machine learning models, and threat intelligence feeds to enhance detection capabilities.

- **Incident Response Layer**: This layer is crucial for developing and executing response plans when security alerts are triggered. Incident response teams are responsible for addressing the detected threats, mitigating damages, and implementing remedial actions.

- **Feedback and Improvement Layer**: After an incident is addressed, lessons learned

- **False Positives**: High rates of false positives can consume resources and distract security teams from genuine threats.

- **Integration Issues**: Difficulty in integrating diverse log sources and formats can hinder effective analysis.

By implementing standardized frameworks, leveraging advanced tools, and refining processes, organizations can overcome these challenges and enhance their overall security monitoring and incident response capabilities.

In conclusion, the security infrastructure of an organization is a complex and dynamic interplay of various components, including SOC architecture, tools and technologies, and log management practices. Establishing a robust SOC is not merely about integrating advanced technologies but also about fostering a culture of continuous improvement and adaptation to the evolving cybersecurity landscape. As cyber threats continue to mount, the importance of a well-structured security infrastructure cannot be overstated. Organizations must invest in the right tools, cultivate skilled personnel, and establish effective processes to ensure they can defend against the myriad of cyber threats they face in the digital age. Through diligence and proactive measures, organizations can not only safeguard their assets but also build resilience against future challenges.

Chapter 4: Monitoring and Incident Analysis

In today's digital landscape, security incidents have become an inevitable part of an organization's operational fabric. This chapter delves into the crucial aspects of monitoring and analyzing security incidents, equipping professionals with the knowledge and techniques needed to enhance their organization's security posture.

4.1 Security Monitoring Techniques

4.1.1 Intrusion Detection Systems (IDS)

Intrusion Detection Systems (IDS) play a pivotal role in security monitoring by detecting unauthorized access or anomalies within the network. IDS can be categorized into two main types: Network-based IDS (NIDS) and Host-based IDS (HIDS).

- **Network-based IDS (NIDS)** monitors network traffic for suspicious activities and alerts administrators. It analyzes data packets, examining headers and payloads for signs of attacks like DDoS, port scanning, or SQL injection.

- **Host-based IDS (HIDS)** is installed on individual hosts, monitoring the inbound and outbound packets as well as system logs and user activities. By analyzing system calls and file integrity, HIDS can detect changes or unauthorized access at the host level.

4.1.2 Security Information and Event Management (SIEM)

SIEM systems aggregate and analyze security data from across the organization's IT environment. By collecting data from servers, network devices, domain controllers, and applications, SIEM tools offer a centralized view of security incidents.

- **Log Management**: SIEM solutions focus heavily on log management, collecting and correlating logs from various sources to detect patterns that may indicate security incidents.

- **Real-time Monitoring**: Advanced SIEM solutions provide real-time monitoring and alerting capabilities, helping security teams respond to incidents as they occur.

- **Compliance and Reporting**: An additional benefit of using SIEM is its ability to assist with regulatory compliance, offering predefined reports that align with standards like GDPR, HIPAA, and PCI-DSS.

4.1.3 User and Entity Behavior Analytics (UEBA)

User and Entity Behavior Analytics (UEBA) enhances traditional monitoring by focusing on the behavior of users and entities within the network. By establishing a baseline of normal behavior and leveraging machine learning algorithms, UEBA can identify deviations that might signal potential threats, such as insider threats or compromised credentials.

- **Behavioral Profiling**: UEBA systems create a comprehensive profile based on user actions, including login patterns, data access, and transaction behaviors.

- **Anomalous Activity Detection**: When a user engages in behavior that deviates significantly from established patterns—like accessing sensitive data at unusual hours or from unfamiliar locations—the UEBA system raises alerts for further investigation.

4.1.4 Threat Hunting

Threat hunting is a proactive security strategy that involves actively searching for undetected threats within the network. Rather than waiting for alerts from automated systems, threat hunters leverage intelligence, experience, and advanced analytics to uncover hidden threats.

- **Hypothesis-driven Approach**: Effective threat hunting often begins with a hypothesis based on intelligence or prior incidents, guiding the search for potential threats.

- **Utilizing Advanced Tools**: Threat hunters typically utilize a variety of tools and techniques, including endpoint detection and response (EDR) systems, forensic tools, and custom scripts to examine unusual behaviors across the environment.

4.2 Security Incident Analysis

4.2.1 Classifying Security Incidents

Before delving into incident analysis, it is critical to classify incidents correctly. Accurate classification aids in understanding the nature of the incident and determining the appropriate response.

- **Types of Incidents**: Security incidents can range from malware infections and data breaches to denial of service attacks and insider threats. Classifying these incidents helps prioritize response actions.

- **Severity Levels**: Assigning severity levels based on the potential impact on the organization guides response efforts. High-severity incidents typically require immediate attention, while lower-severity incidents may warrant a more measured response.

4.2.2 Root Cause Analysis (RCA)

Root Cause Analysis is a systematic approach for identifying the fundamental cause of an incident. It goes beyond symptoms to uncover underlying vulnerabilities or failures within the system or process.

- **Techniques for RCA**: Various methods, such as the "5 Whys" technique or Fishbone diagrams, can facilitate RCA. The goal is to ask "why" multiple times until the root cause is identified.

- **Implementing Lessons Learned**: Following RCA, organizations should implement measures to address the root cause. This could include updating software, adjusting security policies, or enhancing training for employees.

4.2.3 Post-Incident Review

After an incident is contained and analyzed, conducting a post-incident review is essential. This review assesses both the technical and procedural responses to the incident.

- **Incident Response Effectiveness**: Evaluating how effectively the incident response was executed is crucial. This involves reviewing the timeline of events, assessing the adequacy of communication, and identifying gaps in the response.

- **Updating Incident Response Plans**: Insights gleaned from the review should inform updates to the organization's incident response plan, ensuring that it evolves based on real-world experience and lessons learned.

4.3 Optimizing SIEM Rules

A well-configured SIEM can be a powerful tool in the organization's security arsenal.

However, to maximize its efficacy, the optimization of SIEM rules is essential.

4.3.1 Rule Tuning

Overly generic or excessive rules can lead to alert fatigue, where security teams become overwhelmed with alerts, increasing the risk of missing genuine threats.

- **Prioritize High-Fidelity Alerts**: Focus tuning efforts on high-fidelity alerts that have previously shown to indicate true security incidents. This entails reviewing historical incident data to refine rules accordingly.

- **Regular Reviews and Updates**: SIEM rules should not remain static. Regularly reviewing and updating rules in response to evolving threats and business needs is vital for maintaining relevance and effectiveness.

4.3.2 Correlation Rules

Correlation rules combine data from various sources to identify patterns indicative of security incidents. Developing effective correlation rules requires a deep understanding of potential attack vectors and behaviors.

- **Creating Contextual Correlations**: Establish contextual correlations to relate seemingly disparate events, providing deeper insights into potential threats. For instance, if a series of failed login attempts is detected, followed by a successful login from the same IP address, this indicates a potential brute force attack.

- **Integration with Threat Intelligence**: Incorporating threat intelligence into correlation rules can further enhance their efficacy by allowing SIEM systems to correlate internal data with known threats, providing actionable insights.

4.3.3 Custom Dashboards and Reporting

To optimize the use of SIEM tools, organizations should develop custom dashboards that provide relevant insights and metrics. Dashboards can display critical security events, trends over time, and the status of ongoing investigations.

- **Key Performance Indicators (KPIs)**: Establishing and monitoring KPIs specific to security incidents can help organizations gauge their effectiveness in incident response.

- **Automated Reporting**: Automated reporting mechanisms can facilitate compliance efforts, ensuring that necessary information is gathered and reported efficiently.

4.4 Utilizing Threat Intelligence

The effective use of threat intelligence can significantly strengthen an organization's security posture by providing timely information about emerging threats and vulnerabilities.

4.4.1 Types of Threat Intelligence

Threat intelligence can be categorized into three primary types:

- **Strategic Threat Intelligence**: Focused on overarching trends in the cybersecurity landscape, strategic intelligence is typically used by executive leadership for long-term decision-making.

- **Tactical Threat Intelligence**: This type of intelligence focuses on specific threats and tactics employed by adversaries, allowing security teams to develop targeted defenses.

- **Operational Threat Intelligence**: Operational intelligence delves into specific incidents and actor behaviors. This type of intelligence can inform ongoing incident response efforts and real-time defense measures.

4.4.2 Threat Intelligence Platforms (TIPs)

To manage and analyze threat intelligence effectively, organizations increasingly rely on Threat Intelligence Platforms (TIPs). These platforms aggregate data from multiple sources, enabling the correlation and analysis of threat information.

- **Data Aggregation and Normalization**: TIPs collect threat data from various sources, such as open-source intelligence (OSINT), commercial feeds, and shared information from industry groups.

- **Sharing Mechanisms**: TIPs facilitate the sharing of threat intelligence across organizations within the same industry or community, promoting a collective defense strategy.

4.4.3 Integrating Threat Intelligence into Security Operations

Integrating threat intelligence into existing security operations enhances the organization's capabilities in identifying and mitigating threats.

- **Informing Security Policies**: Threat intelligence can inform the development of security policies and best practices, ensuring they are aligned with current threat landscapes.

- **Enhancing Incident Response**: Incorporating threat intelligence into incident response workflows enables security teams to respond more effectively to incidents, drawing on real-time insights about known threats and vulnerabilities.

4.4.4 Measuring the Impact of Threat Intelligence

After implementing threat intelligence initiatives, it is crucial to measure their impact on the organization's security posture.

- **Performance Metrics**: Metrics such as reduced dwell time of threats, improved incident detection rates, and the effectiveness of incident response actions can offer insights into the value gained from threat intelligence.

- **Continuous Improvement**: Utilizing the insights gathered from performance measurement, organizations should continuously refine and enhance their threat intelligence strategies, adapting to the evolving threat landscape.

Chapter 4 emphasized the importance of effective monitoring, thorough incident analysis, optimization of SIEM rules, and the powerful role of threat intelligence in building a robust cybersecurity framework. By understanding and implementing these key components, organizations can better prepare for, detect, and respond to security incidents, ultimately strengthening their overall security posture and resilience against threats. The evolving nature of the digital landscape necessitates ongoing adaptations and improvements—making continuous education, innovation, and vigilance paramount for cybersecurity success.

Through combining advanced monitoring techniques, diligent incident analysis, optimized tools, and actionable intelligence, organizations are poised to not only defend against current threats but to anticipate and mitigate future risks. The journey towards a comprehensive security strategy is ongoing; however, the methods discussed in this chapter provide a pathway for organizations striving to cultivate a safer and more secure environment in an increasingly complex digital world.

Chapter 5: Incident Response Process

The department of information security within any organization is tasked with ensuring the integrity, confidentiality, and availability of information systems and data. One of the critical aspects of this role is effectively managing incidents—unforeseen events that can negatively impact these objectives. This chapter outlines the Incident Response Process, detailing its phases, execution, documentation, and the review that follows an incident.

5.1 Phases of Incident Response

The Incident Response Process is typically divided into several key phases, which, when executed appropriately, help organizations manage and mitigate the effects of an incident. This structured framework ensures that incidents are handled systematically, allowing for effective resolution and comprehensive learning. The phases are as follows:

5.1.1 Preparation

The preparation phase involves establishing and equipping the incident response team (IRT) with the necessary tools, training, and procedures. Key components of preparation include:

- **Policy Development**: Organizations must have well-defined policies regarding incident response, outlining roles and responsibilities, communication protocols, and escalation procedures.

- **Team Training**: Regular training sessions and simulations should be part of the routine to keep the IRT updated on the latest threats and response techniques.

- **Tool Acquisition**: The IRT should be equipped with necessary technologies and resources, such as firewalls, intrusion detection systems, forensic tools, and incident tracking systems.

- **Incident Response Plan**: An incident response plan should be documented, clearly outlining procedures for various types of incidents, including cybersecurity breaches, data loss, and service outages.

5.1.2 Identification

The identification phase involves recognizing and confirming that an incident has occurred. This phase requires vigilant monitoring of systems and networks to detect anomalies. Key activities include:

- **Monitoring**: Continuous monitoring of networks and systems through automated tools enables the early detection of incidents.

- **Incident Reporting**: Employees should have access to reporting mechanisms to escalate suspected incidents.

- **Validation**: Once an incident is reported, the IRT must quickly validate whether the event is indeed an incident and assess its severity.

5.1.3 Containment

Once an incident has been confirmed, containment is crucial to prevent further damage. This phase can be divided into short-term and long-term containment strategies:

- **Short-Term Containment**: Immediate actions are taken to limit the impact of the incident. This might include isolating affected systems or networks from the wider environment.

- **Long-Term Containment**: More strategic measures are implemented to mitigate risks while preparing for recovery. This can involve applying temporary fixes or deploying additional security measures.

5.1.4 Eradication

Eradication involves identifying the root cause of the incident and removing it from the environment to prevent recurrence. Steps include:

- **Root Cause Analysis**: Conducting a thorough analysis to determine how the incident occurred.

- **Malware Removal**: If malware is

involved, it must be eliminated from affected systems.

5.1.5 Recovery

The recovery phase is focused on restoring systems and services to normal operations while ensuring that no vulnerabilities remain. This can involve:

- **System Restoration**: Reinstalling and configuring affected systems as required.

- **Monitoring Post-Recovery**: Keeping a close eye on systems to detect any signs of weaknesses or re-entry of threats.

5.1.6 Lessons Learned

After recovery, it's essential to conduct a

comprehensive review of the incident. This involves gathering the team to reflect on the incident's handling, what went well, what didn't, and how the response process can be improved. This phase is critical for ongoing improvement.

5.2 Executing an Incident Response Plan

The execution of an incident response plan involves putting the planned response measures into action during an incident. Here are the crucial components of effective execution:

5.2.1 Activation of the Incident Response Team

Upon confirmation of an incident, the IRT should be activated without delay. This task includes notifying team members, convening them, and assigning roles and responsibilities based on the incident's scope.

5.2.2 Communicate with Stakeholders

Effective communication during an incident is vital. Stakeholder engagement includes:

- **Internal Communication**: Keeping necessary departments updated on the incident's status, potential impacts, and required actions to take.

- **External Communication**: Depending on the incident severity, it may be necessary to communicate with external stakeholders, including customers, regulators, and media.

5.2.3 Implement Response Procedures

Team members should follow the predefined

protocols within the incident response plan. This process involves documenting actions taken and decisions made throughout the incident.

5.2.4 Coordinate with External Agencies

In severe incidents, organizations may need to involve external agencies such as law enforcement, cybersecurity specialists, or legal counsel. Coordination with these parties should abide by legal and organizational policies to ensure compliance.

5.2.5 Maintain Documentation

Throughout the incident response, meticulous documentation is crucial. This documentation should encompass:

- **Timeline of Events**: A detailed timeline

highlighting key actions and decisions during the event.

- **Incident Evidence**: Gathering and preserving all relevant evidence for new findings and potential legal actions.

5.2.6 Post-Incident Reporting

Following the incident, a comprehensive report should be generated that outlines the event, actions taken, and outcomes. This report should serve multiple purposes, including management reviews and for use in future training and planning.

5.3 Documentation and Reporting of Incidents

Incident documentation and reporting are essential for establishing a clear record of the event and the organization's response. The following elements are essential for effective documentation:

5.3.1 Incident Report Formats

Incident reports should follow a standardized format that includes:

- **Incident Summary**: A brief overview of what happened.

- **Timeline of Events**: A chronological list of actions taken during the incident response.

- **Indicators of Compromise (IoCs)**: Documenting any discovered indicators that could help prevent future occurrences.

- **Impact Analysis**: Assessing the impact,

including any losses or outages experienced.

5.3.2 Evidence Preservation

Collecting and preserving evidence can be crucial for legal proceedings and may help in understanding the incident's cause. Steps to maintain evidence include:

- **Forensic Data Collection**: Employing forensic tools and techniques to secure logs, disk images, and any relevant data.

- **Chain of Custody**: Maintaining clear records of who accessed what data and when to ensure the integrity of evidence.

5.3.3 Communication of Findings

Once incidents are documented, the findings

should be communicated to relevant stakeholders. This process should include:

- **Management Briefings**: Providing a summary report for upper management detailing the incident's impact and response.

- **Team Training**: Utilizing findings from the incident to reinforce training programs and cybersecurity awareness.

5.4 Post-Incident Review and Lessons Learned

The review phase involves critically assessing the incident and the response to identify improvements for future preparedness.

5.4.1 Conducting a Post-Incident Review

Review sessions should involve all members of the IRT and relevant stakeholders. The agenda might cover:

- **What Happened**: Review the incident timeline to understand how it unfolded.

- **Response Effectiveness**: Evaluate the effectiveness of the response strategies employed.

- **Communication**: Review how information was communicated internally and externally.

5.4.2 Identifying Improvements

Identifying weaknesses in the incident response process or gaps in security measures is crucial. Goals of this phase include:

- **Actionable Recommendations**: Generate specific suggestions for improving the incident response plan.

- **Policy Revisions**: Recommend changes to existing policies and protocols based on lessons learned.

5.4.3 Training and Simulations

Incorporating lessons learned into the organization's training agenda ensures continual improvement. Organizations may consider:

- **Update Training Programs**: Modify existing training materials to reflect new insights and best practices from the incident review.

- **Conduct Simulations**: Organizing simulation exercises based on the incident's characteristics to prepare for similar future events.

5.4.4 Report Generation

Finally, a post-incident review report should be developed. This report should be distributed to stakeholders and may include:

- **Executive Summary**: A high-level summary of the incident and its resolution.

- **Recommendations**: Detailed suggestions and next steps for improving the organization's security posture.

- **Follow-Up Actions**: Assign responsibilities for implementing changes based on findings.

In conclusion, the incident response process is vital to an organization's overall risk management strategy. Understanding and implementing a structured response process allows organizations to minimize damage, mitigate risks, and enhance their security posture over time. The investment in preparation, thorough execution during incidents, and comprehensive post-incident analyses is essential in fostering a culture of continuous improvement in incident response capabilities. Through effective management and learning, organizations can better protect their valuable assets and ensure resilience against future incidents.

Chapter 6: Forensic Investigation

6.1 Introduction to Forensic Investigation

Forensic investigation is an essential component of the modern criminal justice system. The term "forensic" derives from the Latin word "forensis," meaning "of the forum," which indicates the use of scientific methods and techniques in legal contexts. Forensic investigation encompasses a wide range of disciplines that work together to identify, collect, preserve, and analyze evidence from crime scenes or related incidents. The primary objective is to obtain reliable information that can assist in solving crimes, prosecuting offenders, and exonerating the innocent.

The field of forensic investigation has grown tremendously in sophistication and scope since its inception. Early forensic techniques were rudimentary and relied heavily on eyewitness testimony and confessions. However, advancements in science and technology have paved the way for a more meticulous and credible approach to criminal investigations. Today, forensic investigators utilize a variety of scientific disciplines, including biology, chemistry, physics, and computer science, to uncover hidden truths and provide critical evidence in legal proceedings.

The importance of forensic investigation cannot be overstated. It plays a pivotal role in solving crimes, ensuring public safety, and maintaining the integrity of the judicial system. Forensic investigators work closely with law enforcement agencies, legal professionals, and other stakeholders to ensure that investigations are conducted systematically and rigorously. Each piece of evidence collected at a crime scene is treated as a potential key to unlocking the mystery behind the crime, and proper handling of this evidence is vital for maintaining its integrity and admissibility in court.

As we delve deeper into the various aspects of forensic investigation, we will explore the processes involved in evidence collection and preservation, the techniques used for forensic analysis, and the tools that aid investigators in their quest for justice. Each of these components is crucial for the successful resolution of criminal cases and speaks to the meticulous and collaborative nature of forensic science.

6.2 Evidence Collection and Preservation

The collection and preservation of evidence are fundamental steps in any forensic investigation. The integrity of the evidence must be maintained to ensure that it is admissible in court and can withstand scrutiny during legal proceedings. This section outlines the procedures and best practices for collecting and preserving evidence in a forensic context.

6.2.1 The Crime Scene: A Controlled

Environment

A crime scene is considered a controlled environment where various types of evidence can be found. This may include physical evidence such as fingerprints, blood, or weapons, as well as trace evidence like hair, fibers, and gunshot residue. The first responders at a crime scene typically include police officers and forensic investigators who must follow established protocols to avoid contamination and loss of evidence.

6.2.2 Securing the Scene

The first step in evidence collection is to secure the crime scene. This involves establishing a perimeter around the area to restrict access and prevent unauthorized individuals from entering. Properly securing the scene helps to maintain the integrity of the evidence and minimizes the risk of contamination. Crime scene tape, cones, or other markers are often used to delineate the boundaries.

6.2.3 Documentation

Thorough documentation of the crime scene is critical. Investigators are required to take detailed notes, photographs, and videos to capture the state of the scene before any evidence is collected or modified. This documentation serves as a permanent record of how the scene appeared immediately after the crime occurred, which can be vital for legal proceedings.

6.2.4 Evidence Collection Techniques

Once the scene is secured and documented, investigators can begin collecting evidence. Various techniques are used depending on the type of evidence:

- **Biological Evidence**: When collecting biological samples like blood or saliva, investigators use sterile containers and gloves to avoid contamination. Swabs are often used to collect samples from surfaces.

- **Physical Evidence**: Items such as weapons, clothing, or personal belongings must be handled with care. Each item should be placed in a separate evidence bag to prevent damage or contamination.

- **Trace Evidence**: Trace evidence, such as hair and fibers, requires specialized techniques for collection. Investigators often use adhesive tape or specialized tools to collect these small particles without losing them.

6.2.5 Chain of Custody

One of the cornerstones of forensic evidence handling is maintaining a clear "chain of custody." This refers to the process of tracking the handling, transfer, and storage of evidence from the moment it is collected until it is presented in court. Each time evidence is handled, a record must be created, detailing who handled the evidence, when it was handled, and what action was taken. A well-documented chain of custody helps ensure that evidence remains credible and reliable throughout the investigative process.

6.2.6 Preservation of Evidence

Evidence preservation is equally important as collection. Various methods are used to ensure that evidence remains intact and uncontaminated throughout the investigation:

- **Proper Storage**: Different types of evidence require specific storage conditions. Biological specimens, for example, may need refrigeration, while physical evidence may need to be kept in a controlled environment to prevent deterioration.

- **Avoiding Contamination**: Investigators must always use gloves and other protective gear when handling evidence to minimize the risk of contamination. Isolated storage can help ensure that evidence does not come into contact with unrelated items.

- **Sealing and Labeling**: Evidence bags must be securely sealed and labeled with pertinent information, such as the date, time, location, and the name of the investigator who collected the evidence. This labeling also includes a unique identifier for tracking purposes.

6.3 Forensic Analysis Techniques

Forensic analysis is the scientific investigation of forensic evidence collected from crime scenes. The techniques employed in forensic analysis depend on the type of evidence being examined. This section highlights several key forensic analysis techniques that are commonly used.

6.3.1 DNA Analysis

One of the most influential advancements in forensic science is DNA analysis. DNA profiling has revolutionized the way investigators link suspects to crimes or exonerate innocent individuals. The process involves several steps:

- **Sample Collection**: Biological samples, such as blood, hair, or skin cells, are collected from the crime scene and sent to a forensic laboratory.

- **Extraction and Amplification**: DNA is

extracted from the sample and amplified using techniques such as Polymerase Chain Reaction (PCR). This allows even tiny amounts of DNA to be analyzed.

- **Profiling**: The DNA profile is generated by analyzing specific regions of the DNA known as loci. The profile is then compared against known samples, such as those from suspects or databases of criminal profiles.

6.3.2 Toxicology

Toxicology analysis is crucial for cases involving suspected overdose, poisoning, or drug-related offenses. Toxicologists analyze biological samples, such as blood or urine, to detect the presence of drugs, alcohol, or other toxic substances. This analysis can provide vital insight into a victim's cause of death or a suspect's state at the time of the crime.

6.3.3 Fingerprint Analysis

Fingerprint identification remains one of the most reliable methods of establishing a person's presence at a crime scene. Forensic experts use techniques such as powder dusting, fuming, or chemical treatment to visualize latent fingerprints. Once discovered, the fingerprints are analyzed and compared against databases of known fingerprints to establish a match.

6.3.4 Ballistics Analysis

In cases involving firearms, ballistics analysis can provide critical evidence. Forensic ballistics experts analyze firearms, ammunition, and the trajectory of bullets to determine details such as the type of weapon used and the distance from which it was fired. This can help reconstruct the events of a shooting and link a crime to a specific firearm.

6.3.5 Digital Forensics

With the rise of technology, digital forensics has emerged as a crucial aspect of forensic investigation. This field involves recovering and analyzing data from electronic devices, such as computers and smartphones. Digital forensics experts use specialized software and techniques to recover deleted files, analyze communication logs, and trace online activities. The information gathered can provide insight into criminal behavior or establish connections between suspects.

6.3.6 Forensic Anthropology

Forensic anthropology involves the examination of human skeletal remains to determine identity, age, sex, and cause of death. Forensic anthropologists use their expertise to analyze bone characteristics and provide invaluable information in cases involving unidentified remains or suspicious deaths.

6.4 Tools for Forensic Investigation

In today's technological landscape, forensic investigators have access to a wide range of tools and equipment that facilitate evidence collection and analysis. This section explores some of the essential tools used in forensic investigations:

6.4.1 Evidence Collection Kits

Forensic investigators utilize evidence collection kits that contain essential tools for gathering different types of evidence. These kits may include gloves, sample bags, swabs, tweezers, brushes for dusting fingerprints, and mortars for collecting trace evidence. Each kit is designed for specific types of evidence to enhance efficiency and minimize contamination.

6.4.2 Forensic Imaging Equipment

High-quality imaging equipment is vital for capturing detailed photographs of crime scenes and evidence. Digital cameras with high-resolution capabilities are commonly used, and forensic photographers often utilize specialized lighting techniques, such as ultraviolet light or polarizing filters, to enhance the visibility of fingerprints or other evidence.

6.4.3 Analytical Instruments

Forensic analysis requires the use of sophisticated analytical instruments, such as gas chromatography-mass spectrometry (GC-MS) for toxicology analysis, DNA sequencers for genetic profiling, and scanning electron microscopes for residue analysis. These instruments allow forensic scientists to precisely analyze complex substances and materials.

6.4.4 Database Systems

Forensic investigators rely on databases to store and analyze evidence. Criminal databases, such as the Combined DNA Index System (CODIS) in the United States, allow law enforcement agencies to compare DNA profiles from crime scenes with known profiles. Similarly, fingerprint databases enable quick comparisons of latent prints to identify potential suspects.

6.4.5 Digital Forensic Tools

Digital forensics tools are specifically designed for recovering and analyzing data from electronic devices. Software applications such as EnCase and FTK allow investigators to perform comprehensive analyses of hard drives, smartphones, and cloud storage, recovering deleted files and analyzing user behavior.

6.4.6 Scene Reconstruction Software

Investigators can use scene reconstruction software to visualize crime scenes and simulate events. These tools use data from crime scene evidence, such as bullet trajectories or dna evidence, to create a detailed digital model of the scene. This reconstruction can provide valuable insights into how a crime occurred and is often used in court presentations.

In conclusion, forensic investigation is a multifaceted process involving the meticulous collection, preservation, and analysis of evidence. Each component, from securing the crime scene to analyzing DNA and employing advanced tools, plays a pivotal role in the pursuit of justice. As forensic science continues to evolve, it offers exciting possibilities for uncovering the truth and enhancing the integrity of legal proceedings. The collaboration between various disciplines within forensic science sets the foundation for solving crimes and ensuring accountability in the criminal justice system.

Chapter 7: Communication and Collaboration (SOC Analyst)

In the evolving landscape of cybersecurity, where threats are becoming increasingly sophisticated, the role of a Security Operations Center (SOC) analyst extends beyond mere technical expertise. The effectiveness of a SOC is highly contingent upon robust communication and collaboration practices both within the team and with external partners. Therefore, this chapter delves into the critical dimensions of communication and collaboration in the SOC environment, addressing internal communication, collaboration with other security teams, and relationship management with external partners.

7.1 Internal Communication within the SOC

Effective internal communication is

foundational for the success of a Security Operations Center. Given the fast-paced and high-stakes nature of cybersecurity, SOC analysts must engage in clear, concise, and consistent communication across various levels of the organization. This involves not just verbal exchanges, but also effective use of digital tools and platforms to streamline information sharing.

7.1.1 Importance of Clear Communication

Clear communication is essential in a SOC, where analysts are frequently required to share incident reports, updates, and findings. Miscommunication can lead to delayed responses to security incidents, potentially allowing threats to escalate. Therefore, SOC teams often implement structured communication protocols, which include standardized reporting templates and regular briefing sessions. These measures ensure that everyone involved has access to the same information and understands the current threat landscape.

7.1.2 Tools and Technologies

A variety of tools facilitate effective internal communication within a SOC. Modern SOCs leverage incident management platforms, ticketing systems, and communication tools such as Slack or Microsoft Teams. These platforms enable real-time communication, ensuring that whenever an incident is detected, relevant team members are notified immediately. Additionally, many SOCs employ dashboards that aggregate data from various sources, allowing analysts to visualize current threats and trends, thus supporting informed discussions.

7.1.3 Regular Team Meetings

Regular team meetings serve as a cornerstone

for internal communication within the SOC. Daily or weekly stand-ups allow SOC analysts to discuss ongoing incidents, share lessons learned, and provide updates on new threats. During these meetings, it is crucial for analysts to communicate not only what they have done but also why certain actions have been taken, fostering a deeper understanding among team members and aiding in collective problem-solving.

7.1.4 Documentation and Knowledge Sharing

In addition to verbal communication, effective documentation is vital in the SOC. Analysts are encouraged to document their procedures, findings, and incident responses meticulously. This documentation serves multiple purposes: it provides a record of past incidents for future reference, it helps in training new analysts, and it contributes to the organization's overall knowledge base. Implementing a Wiki-like solution or a central repository can further enhance knowledge sharing, enabling team members to access and contribute to relevant information easily.

7.1.5 Conflict Resolution and Feedback

In any professional setting, conflicts may arise from differing opinions or stress due to high-stakes situations. Establishing a culture of open dialogue and constructive feedback can help resolve conflicts effectively. Encouraging team members to express their concerns and ideas fosters an environment of trust and collaboration, which is essential for high-pressure scenarios such as incident response.

7.2 Collaboration with Other Security Teams

Collaboration with other teams within an organization's cybersecurity ecosystem is crucial for comprehensive threat detection and response. SOC analysts often work closely with various other security-focused teams, such as Threat Intelligence, Incident Response, and Compliance. Each team contributes unique perspectives and expertise, enhancing the overall security posture of the organization.

7.2.1 Inter-Team Meetings

To foster collaboration, regular inter-team meetings should be scheduled. These meetings provide a platform for teams to update one another on their initiatives, share findings, and discuss ongoing security incidents. By creating a common thread of communication between different teams, organizations can better coordinate their efforts and efficiently tackle security challenges.

7.2.2 Joint Training Sessions

Training sessions that involve multiple security teams can improve collaboration and enhance the skill sets of all involved. Such sessions may cover areas such as threat hunting, incident response scenarios, or specific security technologies. These joint activities help to build relationships among team members, allowing for smoother collaboration during high-pressure incidents.

7.2.3 Cross-Functional Projects

SOC analysts often need to engage in cross-functional projects that require input from various security teams. For example, when developing new security protocols or implementing advanced monitoring tools, collaboration between the SOC, Threat Intelligence, and DevSecOps teams can greatly enhance the effectiveness of these initiatives. Engaging in joint projects not only strengthens relationships but also creates a shared sense of purpose among diverse teams.

7.2.4 Leveraging Intelligence Sharing

Threat intelligence is a crucial component of a SOC's operations, and collaboration with the Threat Intelligence team is critical. By leveraging threat intelligence, SOC analysts can stay informed about emerging threats and vulnerabilities, which allows them to adjust their monitoring efforts proactively. Regular meetings and shared platforms for intelligence dissemination can significantly enhance the analysts' ability to detect and respond swiftly to potential threats.

7.2.5 Incident Response Coordination

During a security incident, collaboration is paramount. The SOC must coordinate closely with Incident Response teams, who may be responsible for containment and remediation. Clear communication and pre-established protocols for incident responses ensure that everyone involved understands their roles and responsibilities, leading to a more streamlined and effective response.

7.3 Managing Relationships with External Partners

In an interconnected world, managing relationships with external partners—such as vendors, service providers, and other organizations—is a vital aspect of a SOC analyst's role. These relationships can provide vital resources, intelligence, and support in the face of cybersecurity threats.

7.3.1 Establishing Trust

Building trust with external partners is essential for effective collaboration. SOC analysts must ensure that communication is transparent and consistent to establish a solid foundation. Regular check-ins and updates on the partnership's status can help maintain this trust.

7.3.2 Collaborative Threat Intelligence Sharing

Many organizations participate in external threat intelligence-sharing platforms, which allow them to share information about emerging threats and vulnerabilities. Active participation in these communities can provide SOC analysts with timely insights into potential threats that may affect their organization. Therefore, establishing and maintaining relationships with these groups is crucial for proactive defense strategies.

7.3.3 Vendor Management

SOC analysts often work closely with technology vendors to ensure that the security tools and software being utilized are performing effectively. This collaboration often involves regular communication regarding updates, vulnerabilities, and patches. Building a good working relationship with vendors is not only beneficial for addressing issues promptly but also enhances the organization's operational efficiency.

7.3.4 External Security Assessments

Working with third-party assessment teams can also enhance an organization's security posture. SOC analysts need to collaborate with external auditors and penetration testing teams to review and improve security policies and practices. Effective communication and the openness to feedback during these assessments can lead to meaningful improvements in the SOC's operations.

7.3.5 Incident Response Collaboration

In scenarios where an incident impacts multiple organizations, collaboration with external partners can be critical. Whether it's sharing information with other SOCs about a common threat or coordinating with law enforcement during a breach, having established trust and effective communication protocols in advance can significantly mitigate damage and streamline resolution efforts.

In conclusion, effective communication and collaboration are essential elements of a successful SOC. Internally, SOC analysts must prioritize clear communication, utilize the right tools, and engage in regular meetings and knowledge sharing. Externally, fostering trust and collaboration with other security teams and partners enhances the overall security posture of the organization. By investing in these practices, SOC analysts can contribute significantly to their organization's resilience against evolving cyber threats.

Chapter 8: Best Practices and Guidelines for a SOC Analyst

As the digital landscape continues to evolve, the importance of having a robust Security Operations Center (SOC) cannot be overstated. The SOC serves as the frontline defense against cyber threats, and its analysts play a crucial role in protecting an organization's assets, data, and reputation. This chapter outlines best practices and guidelines for SOC analysts to enhance their effectiveness, streamline operations, and respond effectively to incidents.

1. Understanding the Role of a SOC Analyst

Before delving into best practices, it is essential to understand the diverse responsibilities of a SOC analyst, which typically include:

- **Monitoring Security Events:** Analysts continuously monitor security alerts and logs to identify potential threats in real time.

- **Incident Response:** SOC analysts are responsible for responding to incidents, investigating breaches, and mitigating vulnerabilities.

- **Threat Hunting:** Proactively searching for threats that may evade traditional detection methods.

- **Reporting:** Generating reports that summarize incidents, analysis, trends, and recommendations for improvement.

- **Maintaining Tools and Technologies:** Keeping security-related tools updated and functioning optimally.

2. Establishing a Strong Foundation

2.1. Defining Objectives and KPIs

It's essential for SOC teams to define clear objectives and Key Performance Indicators (KPIs) to measure their effectiveness. Common KPIs include:

- **Mean Time to Detect (MTTD):** The average time taken to detect a security incident.

- **Mean Time to Respond (MTTR):** The average time taken to respond to and mitigate an incident.

- **Number of Incidents Resolved:** The total number of incidents handled within a specific period.

2.2. Creating a Playbook

A comprehensive incident response playbook is invaluable in guiding analysts through the investigation and resolution process. The playbook should include:

- **Standard Operating Procedures (SOPs):** Clearly defined steps for handling various types of incidents.

- **Escalation Protocols:** Guidelines on when to escalate incidents to higher-level analysts or management.

- **Communication Templates:** Pre-defined templates for communicating with stakeholders during an incident.

2.3. Continuous Training and Education

To stay ahead of evolving threats, SOC analysts must engage in continuous education and training. This includes:

- **Certifications:** Pursuing relevant certifications such as Certified Information Systems Security Professional (CISSP), Certified Incident Handler (GCIH), and CompTIA Security+.

- **Workshops and Conferences:** Attending industry conferences (e.g., Black Hat, DEFCON) and local workshops to learn about new tools, techniques, and threats.

- **Knowledge Sharing:** Encouraging a culture of knowledge sharing within the SOC team to enhance collective expertise.

3. Effective Monitoring Practices

3.1. Utilizing Advanced SIEM Solutions

Security Information and Event Management (SIEM) solutions aggregate and analyze security data from across the organization. Best practices for using SIEM solutions include:

- **Fine-Tuning Alerts:** Configuring alerts based on the organization's threat landscape and acceptable risk levels to minimize false positives.

- **Log Management:** Regularly reviewing and archiving logs to comply with regulatory requirements and facilitate investigations.

3.2. Threat Intelligence Integration

Incorporating threat intelligence feeds into SOC operations can improve detection capabilities significantly. Analysts should:

- **Stay Updated:** Regularly update threat intelligence feeds to stay informed about the latest threat actors and tactics.

- **Tailor Intelligence to Environment:** Customize threat intelligence feeds to focus on specific threats relevant to the organization.

4. Incident Response Best Practices

4.1. Follow the Incident Response Lifecycle

SOC analysts should adhere to the incident response lifecycle, which includes:

1. **Preparation:** Ensuring that the SOC is equipped with the necessary tools, playbooks,

and protocols.

2. **Detection and Analysis:** Identifying potential incidents and analyzing the severity of the threat.

3. **Containment, Eradication, and Recovery:** Taking immediate actions to contain the threat, eradicate it from the environment, and recover systems to normal operations.

4. **Post-Incident Review:** Conducting a thorough post-incident review to identify lessons learned and improve future responses.

4.2. Effective Communication

Maintaining clear communication during incidents is critical. Analysts should:

- **Establish Clear Roles:** Define roles and responsibilities during incidents to avoid confusion and streamline the response process.

- **Engage Stakeholders:** Keep management and other relevant departments informed about the status of incidents and actions taken.

5. Threat Hunting and Proactive Defense

5.1. Employing Threat Hunting Techniques

Threat hunting involves proactively searching for threats that may not be detected by traditional security measures. Successful threat hunting practices include:

- **Hypothesis-Driven Approaches:**
Formulating hypotheses based on threat
intelligence and existing vulnerabilities to
guide investigations.

- **Utilizing Behavioral Analysis:**
Monitoring for anomalies in user and entity
behavior to identify potential threats.

5.2. Continuous Improvement

SOC analysts should constantly strive for
improvement by:

- **Reviewing and Analyzing Logs:**
Regularly conducting log analysis to identify
unusual patterns or trends.

- **Iterative Approach:** Treating threat
hunting as a continuous cycle of learning and
adapting based on findings.

6. Collaboration and Information Sharing

6.1. Building Relationships with Other Teams

Collaboration with other departments, such as IT, legal, and compliance, is vital for a successful SOC. Analysts should:

- **Conduct Joint Training:** Engage in joint training sessions with other teams to foster a better understanding of processes and expectations.

- **Regular Meetings:** Schedule regular meetings to discuss current security challenges and collaborate on solutions.

6.2. Sharing Threat Intelligence

Participating in information-sharing initiatives and organizations (e.g., Information Sharing and Analysis Centers - ISACs) allows SOC analysts to stay informed about emerging threats.

7. Documentation and Reporting

7.1. Maintaining Comprehensive Documentation

Documentation is vital for tracking security incidents and ensuring compliance. Analysts should:

- **Document Incidents Thoroughly:** Record every step taken during an incident response for future reference and analysis.

- **Create Knowledge Databases:** Develop a repository of past incidents and lessons learned to guide future responses.

7.2. Regular Reporting

Regular reporting helps stakeholders understand the state of the organization's security posture. Analysts should:

- **Provide Summaries to Management:** Create executive summaries that highlight key metrics, trends, and recommendations.

- **Conduct Detailed Reports:** Prepare in-depth reports for technical teams, outlining findings, actions, and proposed enhancements.

8. Mental Health and Stress Management

8.1. Recognizing Burnout

SOC analysts often operate in high-pressure environments, which can lead to burnout. It is crucial to recognize signs of stress and burnout, such as:

- Increased fatigue and irritability.

- A noticeable drop in performance.

- Loss of interest in routine tasks.

8.2. Promoting Work-Life Balance

Organizations should promote a healthy work-life balance by:

- **Encouraging Time Off:** Encourage analysts to take regular breaks and utilize vacation days.

- **Implementing Flexible Schedules:**
Offering flexible work hours to accommodate personal needs and reduce stress.

In conclusion, becoming an effective SOC analyst requires a combination of technical skills, industry knowledge, and best practices. By adhering to the guidelines presented in this chapter, analysts can optimize their operations, enhance their incident response capabilities, and contribute significantly to the organization's overall security posture. Continuous education, effective communication, collaboration, and a focus on mental health are essential in navigating the ever-evolving and challenging landscape of cybersecurity.

With the right practices in place, SOC analysts can serve as the backbone of an organization's defense strategy, effectively mitigating risks and protecting critical assets from cyber threats. As threats continue to grow in sophistication, the role of the SOC analyst will remain paramount in safeguarding digital environments and maintaining organizational integrity.

Chapter 9: A Comprehensive Guide to Using Splunk

Splunk is a powerful tool for searching, analyzing, and visualizing machine-generated data in real time. This chapter aims to provide a detailed step-by-step guide on how to effectively use Splunk, from installation through to advanced data analysis techniques. This guide is intended for both beginners and experienced users looking to deepen their understanding of Splunk's capabilities.

Section 1: Introduction to Splunk

1.1 What is Splunk?

Splunk is a software platform widely used for monitoring, searching, analyzing, and visualizing machine-generated data in various formats. It enables users to understand the data generated by their systems and get insights into system performance, security, user activity, and much more.

1.2 Key Features of Splunk

- **Data Ingestion:** Splunk can ingest data from a variety of sources, including logs, configurations, and event data.

- **Powerful Search:** The search capabilities are based on the Search Processing Language (SPL), which allows complex queries on large datasets.

- **Visualization:** Splunk provides various visualization tools like charts, dashboards, and reports to represent data graphically.

- **Alerts and Reports:** Users can create alerts based on specific conditions and generate periodic reports.

- **Machine Learning:** Splunk supports machine learning functionalities for predictive analytics.

1.3 Use Cases

Some of the common use cases for Splunk include the following:

- **IT Operations Management:** Monitoring system logs and ensuring performance.
- **Security Information and Event Management (SIEM):** Analyzing security events and incidents.
- **Business Analytics:** Monitoring user activity to improve business processes.

Section 2: Installing Splunk

2.1 System Requirements

Before installing Splunk, ensure that your

system meets the following requirements:

- Supported operating systems: Windows, Linux, or MacOS.

- Minimum of 8 GB RAM.

- At least 20 GB of free disk space.

- A supported web browser for accessing the Splunk Web interface.

2.2 Downloading Splunk

1. Navigate to the [Splunk Download Page] (https://www.splunk.com/en_us/download.ht ml).

2. Choose the appropriate version of Splunk for your operating system.

3. Download the installation package.

2.3 Installing Splunk on Windows

1. Double-click the downloaded `.msi` file.

2. Follow the on-screen instructions. Choose 'Next' to proceed through the installation wizard.

3. Agree to the license agreement.

4. Choose the installation directory (default is usually fine).

5. Configure the administrator account by setting a username and password.

6. Choose to install it as a service.

7. Complete the installation process.

2.4 Installing Splunk on Linux

1. Open a terminal window.

2. Run the following command to install Splunk:

```
```

sudo dpkg -i splunk_package_name.deb # For Debian-based systems

sudo rpm -ivh splunk_package_name.rpm # For Red Hat-based systems

```
```

3. After installation, navigate to the Splunk installation directory:

```
```

cd /opt/splunk/bin

```
```

4. Start Splunk:

```
```

sudo ./splunk start

```
```

5. Follow the prompts to accept the license agreement and set the admin password.

2.5 Starting Splunk

After the installation, open a web browser and go to:

```

http://localhost:8000

```

Log in using the credentials created during the installation process.

Section 3: Configuring Your Splunk Environment

3.1 Adding Data to Splunk

1. Once logged into Splunk, navigate to the **Settings** menu.

2. Click on **Add Data**.

3. Choose the method for adding data (e.g., Upload, Monitor, or Forward).

3.1.1 Uploading Files

- Select `Upload` to upload files from your local machine.

- Click `Select file` and navigate to your file location.

- Follow the prompts to specify the source type and index.

3.1.2 Monitoring Files and Directories

- Choose `Monitor` to monitor log files or directories.

- Specify the paths of files or folders you want to ingest.

- Assign a source type or let Splunk determine it.

3.2 Configuring Indexes

Indexes in Splunk are where data is stored. By default, Splunk creates an index called `main`. You can create additional custom indexes:

1. Go to **Settings** > **Indexes**.

2. Click on **New Index**.

3. Enter the index name and configure the parameters as needed.

4. Save the new index.

3.3 Setting up User Roles and Permissions

1. Go to **Settings** > **Users and Authentication** > **Roles**.

2. Click on **Create Role** to define roles with specific access levels.

3. Assign capabilities to the role based on what users in that role need to access.

Section 4: Searching in Splunk

4.1 Basic Search

1. In the Splunk search bar, input simple queries to find information.

2. For example, to search for events that include the word "error":

```
error
```

3. Press Enter to execute the search.

4.2 Using Search Processing Language (SPL)

- Explore the structure of SPL through basic commands.

4.2.1 Filtering Results

Use commands like `search`, `fields`, and `where` to filter:

```
index=main error
| fields user, timestamp
| where status="failed"
```

4.2.2 Sorting and Limiting Results

To sort or limit the output:

```
| sort - timestamp
```

| head 10

```
```

4.3 Saving and Sharing Searches

1. After conducting a search, click on **Save As**.

2. Choose to save it as a report, alert, or Dashboard panel.

3. Share the link or provide access to relevant users.

Section 5: Visualizing Data

5.1 Creating Charts and Graphs

To visualize your search results, you can create various types of charts:

1. Execute a SPL query.

2. In the results tab, select the **Visualization** option.

3. Choose the type of chart you want (Bar, Line, Pie, etc.).

5.2 Building Dashboards

1. Go to **Dashboards** and select **Create New Dashboard**.

2. Name your dashboard and choose the layout.

3. Add panels based on existing reports or saved searches.

5.3 Using Dashboard Studio

Splunk provides a more advanced platform called Dashboard Studio for creating more customizable dashboards. Here, you can use a graphical interface to arrange and design dashboards easily.

Section 6: Setting Up Alerts

6.1 Creating Alerts

1. After running a search, click on **Save As** and select **Alert**.

2. Define the alert conditions (e.g., if results are greater than 10).

3. Set up actions, such as sending an email or running a script.

6.2 Managing Alerts

1. Go to **Settings** > **Searches, Reports, and Alerts**.

2. Here you can enable, disable, or edit alerts

as needed.

Section 7: Utilizing Machine Learning

7.1 Introduction to Machine Learning in Splunk

Splunk allows data scientists and analysts to leverage machine learning algorithms to uncover patterns within their data more effectively.

1. Navigate to the **Machine Learning Toolkit**.

2. Explore pre-built models for various applications like anomaly detection, classification, and regression.

7.2 Training a Machine Learning Model

1. Use the appropriate Splunk commands.

2. Collect and prepare your data.

3. Apply a machine learning algorithm.

4. Validate and evaluate the model's performance.

Section 8: Advanced Data Analysis

8.1 Using Stats Commands

Use SPL `stats` commands to aggregate or summarize your data:

```
index=main
| stats count by user
```

8.2 Correlation Searches

Correlation searches can help link different types of data based on criteria you define.

1. Create a search query that combines multiple indices.

2. Use the `join` command if necessary.

Section 9: Best Practices

- **Organize Data:** Use indexes and source types effectively to manage your data.

- **Documenting Searches:** Always document your SPL queries for future reference.

- **Manage User Permissions:** Regularly review and update user roles and permissions to maintain security.

Conclusion

Using Splunk effectively requires understanding its vast array of features and best practices. By following the steps outlined in this guide, you can leverage Splunk to gain valuable insights from your machine-generated data, thereby making informed decisions based on real-time analyses.

Chapter 10: Guide to Using Palo Alto Networks Cortex XSOAR

Introduction

Palo Alto Networks Cortex XSOAR (Security Orchestration, Automation, and Response) is a comprehensive platform designed to facilitate the automation of security operations and incident response processes. In this chapter, we'll provide a detailed guide on how to effectively use Cortex XSOAR, including step-by-step instructions for setting up, configuring, and utilizing the platform.

Table of Contents

1. **Understanding Cortex XSOAR**

   - 1.1 Overview

   - 1.2 Key Features

5. **Advanced Features**

   - 5.1 Threat Intelligence

   - 5.2 Reporting and Analytics

   - 5.3 Customizing Cortex XSOAR

6. **Best Practices**

   - 6.1 Optimizing Performance

   - 6.2 User Training and Support

7. **Conclusion**

---

1. Understanding Cortex XSOAR

1.1 Overview

Cortex XSOAR is an innovative platform that integrates various security tools and processes, allowing organizations to streamline their security operations. By automating repetitive tasks and orchestrating multiple technologies, Cortex XSOAR helps security teams respond to incidents faster and more efficiently.

1.2 Key Features

- **Playbook Automation**: Automate repetitive security tasks to save time and reduce the potential for human error.

- **Incident Management**: Streamline the process of managing security incidents from detection to resolution.

- **Threat Intelligence**: Integrate threat intelligence feeds to enhance decision-making during incident response.

- **Collaboration Tools**: Foster collaboration among security team members during incidents through centralized communication channels.

1.3 Benefits

Using Cortex XSOAR offers numerous benefits, including improved incident response times, reduced workload for security professionals, enhanced visibility into security operations, and an overall increase in organizational security posture.

2. Getting Started

2.1 System Requirements

Before installing Cortex XSOAR, ensure that your environment meets the following system requirements:

- **Operating System**: Ubuntu or another supported Linux distribution.

- **Memory**: At least 16 GB of RAM is recommended.

- **CPU**: Multi-core processor with a minimum of 4 cores.

- **Disk Space**: At least 200 GB of available disk space.

2.2 Installation

To install Cortex XSOAR, follow these steps:

1. **Download Installer**: Obtain the installation package from the Palo Alto Networks website.

2. **Access Command Line**: Open a terminal on your server.

3. **Run Installer**: Navigate to the directory where the installer is located and run the

following command:

```bash
sudo ./install.sh
```

4. **Follow Prompts**: The installer will prompt you for various configurations. Follow the on-screen instructions to complete the installation.

2.3 Initial Setup

Once installed, perform the initial setup:

1. **Access the Web Interface**: Open a web browser and navigate to the URL provided during installation, typically `https://<your_server_ip>:443`.

2. **Create Admin Account**: The first time you access the platform, you will be prompted to create an admin account. Fill in required fields and set a secure password.

3. **Configure Initial Settings**: Set up basic configurations, including timezone, language, and other preferences.

3. Configuration

3.1 Integrating with Security Tools

Cortex XSOAR supports integration with numerous security tools. To integrate:

1. **Navigate to Integrations**: Click on the "Integrations" tab in the main menu.

2. **Select Apps**: Browse through the list of available integration apps and click on the one you wish to configure.

3. **Input Credentials**: Enter the necessary credentials and configuration settings for the selected tool.

4. **Test Connection**: Use the "Test" button to ensure the integration is functioning correctly.

5. **Save Settings**: Click "Save" to finish the integration.

3.2 Configuring Playbooks

Playbooks are essential in Cortex XSOAR, automating responses to specific incidents:

1. **Access Playbooks**: Go to the "Automations" tab and select "Playbooks".

2. **Create New Playbook**: Click on "Create New Playbook" to start designing a new automation process.

3. **Define Steps**: Drag and drop various tasks and decision points onto the canvas to

design your playbook.

4. **Configure Tasks**: For each task, click to open its configuration and set required parameters.

5. **Save and Test**: After creating the playbook, save it and run a test to ensure it performs as expected.

3.3 User Management

Proper user management is crucial for maintaining security and efficiency:

1. **Access User Management**: Click on the "User Management" tab from the main menu.

2. **Add New User**: Click on "Add User" and input user information, including username, email, and role assignments.

3. **Set Permissions**: Define the permissions and access levels for each user

based on their responsibilities.

4. **Save**: Click "Save" to create the user account.

4. Using Cortex XSOAR

4.1 Dashboard Overview

The dashboard is your primary interface for monitoring security operations:

1. **Access Dashboard**: Log in to Cortex XSOAR and navigate to the dashboard.

2. **View Widgets**: Familiarize yourself with the various widgets that display real-time data on incidents, alerts, and system health.

3. **Customize Layout**: Personalize the dashboard layout by adding or removing widgets based on your preferences.

4.2 Case Management

Effectively managing security cases is crucial for incident resolution:

1. **Create a New Case**: Click on "New Case" from the Cases tab.

2. **Input Details**: Fill in incident details, prioritizing key information such as severity and affected systems.

3. **Assign Analysts**: Assign team members to the case based on their expertise.

4. **Track Progress**: Use the case management interface to track the progress and communicate with team members through comments and updates.

4.3 Automation Playbooks

Automation playbooks save time and reduce

manual errors:

1. **Access Automation Tab**: Navigate to the "Automations" section and select "Playbooks".

2. **Run Existing Playbook**: Choose from available playbooks and click "Run".

3. **Monitor Execution**: View real-time updates on the execution status and results of the playbook.

4. **Analyze Outcomes**: Post-execution, analyze the results to refine playbooks for future incidents.

4.4 Incident Response

Responding to security incidents promptly is critical:

1. **Identify Incidents**: Use the dashboard

to identify alerts and potential incidents.

2. **Assess Severity**: Evaluate the severity and impact of each incident.

3. **Engage Response Teams**: Collaborate with security analysts by utilizing the chat feature to coordinate responses.

4. **Execute Playbooks**: Utilize predefined playbooks to automate parts of the incident response process.

5. Advanced Features

5.1 Threat Intelligence

Incorporating threat intelligence enhances your organization's security posture:

1. **Access Threat Intelligence**: Navigate to the "Threat Intelligence" section.

2. **Integrate Feeds**: Configure and

integrate external threat intelligence feeds to improve incident context.

3. **Review Intelligence**: Regularly review threat intelligence for actionable insights that could impact security operations.

5.2 Reporting and Analytics

Generate reports to provide insights into security operations:

1. **Navigate to Reporting**: Go to the "Reports" section from the main menu.

2. **Create New Report**: Click on "Create Report" and select parameters to include in the report.

3. **Schedule Reports**: Optionally, configure the report to run on a periodic basis and be emailed to relevant stakeholders.

4. **Analyze Data**: Use generated reports to analyze trends and inform security strategy.

5.3 Customizing Cortex XSOAR

Customization allows you to tailor Cortex XSOAR to your organization's needs:

1. **Access Settings**: Click on the "Settings" tab.

2. **Customize Layouts**: Adjust the UI layout to match the workflows of your security team.

3. **Develop Custom Integrations**: Use the development tools available in Cortex XSOAR to build custom integrations for your specific tools.

6. Best Practices

6.1 Optimizing Performance

To ensure smooth operation, follow these best

practices:

- Regularly update the platform to the latest version.

- Monitor system performance and resource usage to address bottlenecks promptly.

- Archive old data periodically to keep the database manageable.

6.2 User Training and Support

Ensuring your team is well-trained is essential:

- Conduct regular training sessions on using Cortex XSOAR.

- Create documentation and resources for users to reference.

- Establish a support process for users encountering issues.

Palo Alto Networks Cortex XSOAR offers comprehensive capabilities for security orchestration, automation, and response. By setting up the platform correctly and utilizing its features effectively, your organization can enhance its security posture and streamline incident response processes. Follow the steps outlined in this guide to maximize the benefits of Cortex XSOAR in your security operations.

Chapter 11: Guide to Using Cisco Firepower

Cisco Firepower is a comprehensive security solution that provides advanced threat protection through its integrated threat defense capabilities. This guide will take you through the steps to deploy, configure, and manage Cisco Firepower effectively. We will cover everything from initial setup to advanced features and troubleshooting tips.

Section 1: Understanding Cisco Firepower

Before diving into the usage of Cisco Firepower, it's essential to understand its key components:

1. **Firepower Management Center (FMC)**: This is the centralized management system for Firepower devices. It allows for policy management, logging, reporting, and

analysis of network traffic.

2. **Firepower Threat Defense (FTD)**: This is the software that runs on Cisco devices to provide intrusion prevention, URL filtering, advanced malware protection, and more.

3. **Firepower Devices**: These are the hardware appliances or virtual devices that incorporate the Firepower features.

Section 2: Prerequisites

Before starting with the configuration, ensure you have:

- A Cisco Firepower device (hardware or virtual).

- A Firepower Management Center (either dedicated or in the cloud).

- The necessary network connectivity and

access.

- Basic understanding of networking concepts and security appliances.

Section 3: Initial Setup

Step 1: Connecting to Your Firepower Device

1. **Physical Connection**: Connect your computer to the Firepower device using an Ethernet cable. Use the management port for the initial configuration.

2. **Power On the Device**: Ensure the device is powered on and allow it to boot up.

3. **Access the CLI**: Use a terminal emulator (like PuTTY) to connect to the device's console. Set the appropriate settings

(usually: 9600 baud rate, 8 data bits, no parity, 1 stop bit).

Step 2: Configuring Basic Settings

1. **Initial Configuration Wizard**: Upon first boot, you may be prompted with an initial configuration wizard. Follow these prompts to set up basic configurations like:

   - **Management IP Address**: Assign a static IP address to the management interface.

   - **Subnet Mask**: Specify the subnet mask for the management network.

   - **Gateway**: Set the default gateway.

2. **Admin Password**: Set a strong password for the admin user account.

3. **DNS Settings**: Configure the DNS

settings for external name resolution.

4. **NTP Configuration**: Optional but recommended to synchronize time, which is critical for logs.

5. **Save Configuration**: Once you've completed the initial setup, ensure to save your configuration.

Step 3: Accessing Firepower Management Center

1. **Open a Web Browser**: Use your preferred web browser to access the Firepower Management Center by entering its IP address.

2. **Login**: Use the credentials established during the initial setup to log in.

3. **Dashboard Overview**: Familiarize yourself with the dashboard, which provides insights into threats, incidents, and overall security posture.

Section 4: Configuring Policies

Step 1: Creating Access Control Policies

1. **Navigate to Policies**: In the FMC dashboard, go to the 'Policies' tab.

2. **Access Control Policy**: Click on 'Access Control' and select 'Access Control Policies'.

3. **New Policy**: Click 'Add Policy', give it a descriptive name, and select the appropriate settings (like the type of policy: Prevent, Monitor).

4. **Adding Rules**: Within the policy, you'll want to add rules by clicking 'Add Rule'. Define conditions like:

  - **Source/Destination**: Specify IP ranges or hosts.

  - **Applications**: Include or exclude specific applications.

  - **URL Categories**: Filter web traffic based on categories.

5. **Actions**: For each rule, specify the action (Permit, Deny, or Monitor).

6. **Save the Policy**: Ensure to save your newly created access control policy.

Step 2: Setting Up Intrusion Policies

1. **Navigate Back to Policies**: Go to 'Policies' again in the FMC.

2. **Intrusion Policies**: Click on 'Intrusion Prevention' to access intrusion policies.

3. **New Intrusion Policy**: Click 'Add Policy'; configure it based on your security requirements.

4. **Select Snort Rules**: Choose the appropriate Snort rules that fit your network environment.

5. **Tuning and Thresholds**: Adjust the thresholds and tuning settings to reduce false positives while maintaining strong security.

6. **Apply and Save**: Once the

configuration is done, apply it and save your settings.

Section 5: Logging and Monitoring

Step 1: Setting Up Logging

1. **Navigate to System Settings**: Under the 'System' tab, access 'Logging' settings.

2. **Configure Logging Levels**: Decide what types of logs you want to keep (INFO, WARN, ERROR, etc.).

3. **Log Destination**: Choose where to send the log data – to FMC, an external syslog server, or a combination.

4. **Save Settings**: Make sure to save after making changes.

Step 2: Monitoring Traffic

1. **Access the Monitoring Tab**: In FMC, go to the 'Monitoring' section.

2. **Traffic Analysis**: Use the 'Traffic' sub-tab to analyze current traffic patterns, review connections, and identify active sessions.

3. **Review Events**: Look into 'Incidents' to check for alerts and threat notifications.

4. **Creating Reports**: Generate reports by navigating to 'Reports', and create custom reports based on incidents, alerts, and traffic statistics.

Section 6: Advanced Features
Step 1: Integrating Threat Intelligence

1. **Access Threat Intelligence Settings**: In FMC, go to 'System' and then 'Integration' to setup threat intelligence feeds.

2. **Add Threat Feeds**: Configure external threat feeds that the Firepower device can use to update its threat database.

3. **Test and Validate**: Ensure that the threat intelligence feed is operational and updating correctly.

Step 2: Utilizing Advanced Malware Protection (AMP)

1. **AMP Configuration**: Under the 'Policies' tab, enable and configure AMP settings for devices to scan uploads, downloads, and activities.

2. **File Policies**: Create file policies that define how files should be analyzed (sandboxing, reputation, etc.).

3. **Monitor AMP Events**: In the monitoring tab, check for AMP-related events for malicious files or activities.

Step 3: Managing VPNs

1. **Setting Up VPN**: Navigate to the 'Devices' section, select your device, and go to the 'VPN' tab.

2. **Add a New VPN Configuration**: Configure IKEv2 or other VPN types as needed.

3. **Specify Parameters**: Define the parameters for authentication, encryption, and session management.

4. **Save and Apply**: After verifying that all settings are correct, save it and apply the changes.

Section 7: Troubleshooting and Best Practices

Step 1: Common Troubleshooting Steps

1. **Check Connectivity**: Ensure that all network interfaces are up and configured correctly.

2. **Review Logs**: Check system logs to identify any unusual behavior or errors.

3. **Validate Policies**: Sometimes policies may be too strict, causing legitimate traffic to be blocked. Review and adjust accordingly.

4. **Use the CLI**: Familiarize yourself with

the command line interface for deeper troubleshooting, including commands like `show version`, `show ip interface`, etc.

Step 2: Best Practices

1. **Regular Updates**: Ensure that both the Firepower device and FMC are regularly updated for the latest features and security patches.

2. **Review Policies Periodically**: Conduct periodic reviews and adjustments of your security policies to adapt to evolving threats.

3. **Conduct Security Audits**: Regular audits will help in identifying weaknesses in your setup.

4. **Backup Configurations**: Regularly backup device configurations and logs for

disaster recovery and compliance.

Using Cisco Firepower effectively requires understanding its components, configuring them correctly, monitoring performance, and keeping everything updated. This guide has provided a detailed walkthrough from initial setups to advanced features and troubleshooting techniques, ensuring that you are equipped to handle the security needs in a dynamic network environment. As the threat landscape evolves, continuous learning and adapting your Firepower deployment will be essential in maintaining a robust security posture.

Chapter 12: Complete Guide to Palo Alto Networks

In this chapter, we will explore Palo Alto Networks (PAN), a leading cybersecurity company known for its advanced firewall technology and comprehensive security solutions. We will cover the main features and functionalities of Palo Alto Networks' products, focusing on how to implement and manage them effectively in your organization. This guide will be divided into several sections to provide a step-by-step approach that will help you understand and utilize Palo Alto Networks' offerings.

Section 1: Introduction to Palo Alto Networks

Palo Alto Networks is a cybersecurity company that provides a wide range of products and services designed to protect organizations from cyber threats. Their main offerings include next-generation firewalls (NGFWs), cloud security, endpoint protection, and threat intelligence services. With the increasing complexity of cyber threats, organizations must have a robust and proactive cybersecurity strategy, making PAN a valuable partner in this endeavor.

1.1 Why Choose Palo Alto Networks?

1. **Next-Generation Firewall**: PAN's NGFW provides deep packet inspection, application awareness, and user identification, allowing for precise control over traffic.

2. **Comprehensive Security Solutions**: From endpoint protection to cloud security, PAN offers an integrated approach to cybersecurity.

3. **Threat Intelligence**: PAN's threat intelligence services can help organizations stay ahead of emerging threats.

1.2 Overview of Palo Alto Products

1. **Palo Alto Firewalls**: These devices provide network security and traffic management capabilities, protecting against cyber threats.

2. **Prisma Cloud**: A cloud-native security platform that offers comprehensive security for cloud applications.

3. **Cortex**: An AI-driven security operations platform that enhances threat detection and response capabilities.

4. **GlobalProtect**: A VPN solution that secures remote access to an organization's resources.

Section 2: Getting Started with Palo Alto Networks

This section will guide you through the process of getting started with Palo Alto

Networks products. We will focus on setting up a Palo Alto firewall, which is one of the most common entry points for organizations looking to enhance security.

2.1 Initial Setup of Palo Alto Firewalls

Step 1: Unboxing and Physical Installation

1. **Unbox the Firewall**: Carefully unbox the device and ensure all components are included: the firewall unit, power supply, and documentation.

2. **Mount the Device**: If necessary, install the firewall in a rack or on a shelf, ensuring proper airflow and clearance.

3. **Connect Power**: Connect the power supply to the firewall and plug it into a power source.

4. **Network Connections**: Connect the

firewall to your network using Ethernet cables. The cable should connect the WAN port to your internet source and the LAN ports to your internal network.

Step 2: Accessing the Firewall Interface

1. **Initial Connection**: Connect your computer to one of the LAN ports using an Ethernet cable.

2. **Set IP Address**: Manually configure your computer's IP address to be in the same subnet as the default IP address of the firewall (typically 192.168.1.1).

3. **Access the Web Interface**: Open a web browser and enter the firewall's default IP address (usually https://192.168.1.1).

4. **Login Credentials**: Use the default administrator credentials (admin/admin) to log in.

Step 3: Initial Configuration Wizard

1. **Run the Wizard**: Upon first login, you will be prompted to run the setup wizard, which will guide you through the initial configuration.

2. **Configuration Steps**: Set the device management and data interfaces, configure the timezone, and set the administrator password.

3. **Configure Interfaces**: Specify the IP addresses for the WAN and LAN interfaces and enable the necessary zones.

4. **Save Settings**: Review your settings and save the configuration.

2.2 Licensing and Update Configuration

Before using the firewall, it is crucial to obtain the necessary licenses and ensure the device is up-to-date.

Step 1: Licensing

1. **Select Licensing Options**: Choose the licenses you need based on your organization's requirements. Common licenses include Threat Prevention, URL Filtering, and WildFire.

2. **Activate Licenses**: Log in to the Palo Alto Networks Customer Support Portal. Navigate to the Licenses section and activate the required licenses by entering the serial number of the firewall.

Step 2: Updating the Device

1. **Check for Updates**: In the firewall web interface, navigate to Device > Software and check for any available updates.

2. **Install Updates**: Download and install the latest updates to ensure your device has the latest features and security patches.

Section 3: Configuring Security Policies

In this section, we will detail how to create and manage security policies to protect your network. Security policies are essential for controlling inbound and outbound traffic based on specific criteria.

3.1 Understanding Security Policies

1. **Security Rules Overview**: Security rules define how traffic is handled based on source/destination IP addresses, applications, users, and schedules.

2. **Concept of Zones**: Zones are logical groupings of interfaces that simplify policy management. Common zones include "Trust," "Untrust," and "DMZ."

3.2 Creating Security Policies

Step 1: Create a New Security Policy

189

1. **Navigate to Policies**: Go to the Policies tab in the Palo Alto Networks web interface.

2. **Add a Policy Rule**: Click on the 'Add' button to create a new security rule.

3. **Define Rule Criteria**: Specify the source zone, destination zone, application, and user/group.

4. **Action Selection**: Choose the action (allow or deny) for the matching traffic.

Step 2: Logging and Notifications

1. **Enable Logging**: Ensure you enable logging for the policy to track hits and analyze traffic.

2. **Set Notifications**: Configure alerts to notify the security team of critical events.

3.3 Policy Order and Best Practices

1. **Policy Order**: Remember that policies are processed in order from top to bottom; more specific rules should be placed above more general ones.

2. **Review and Audit**: Regularly review and audit security policies to ensure they remain effective and relevant to your organization's changing needs.

Section 4: Monitoring and Logging

Effective monitoring and logging are crucial for maintaining a secure environment. In this section, we'll explore how to monitor traffic and analyze logs.

4.1 Traffic Monitoring

1. **View Monitor Tab**: Navigate to the Monitor tab in the web interface to access various monitoring tools.

2. **Live Traffic**: Use the "Traffic" option to view real-time traffic passing through the firewall.

3. **Filtering and Searching**: Utilize filters to search for specific traffic patterns or events, including IP addresses, applications, and users.

4.2 Log Management

1. **Log Types Overview**: Familiarize yourself with different log types, including Traffic, Threat, and System logs.

2. **Export Logs**: You can export logs for external analysis or long-term storage by navigating to the "Logs" section and selecting the desired logs to export.

3. **Create Custom Reports**: Use the reporting feature to create customized reports

for analysis and compliance purposes.

Section 5: Advanced Features and Integrations

Palo Alto Networks firewalls offer several advanced features that can further enhance your organization's security posture.

5.1 Threat Prevention

1. **Enable Threat Prevention**: Navigate to the Device > Threat Prevention tab and enable threat prevention features such as Antivirus, Anti-Spyware, and Vulnerability Protection.

2. **Regular Updates**: Ensure that threat signatures are updated regularly by configuring automatic updates.

5.2 User-ID and Application Identification

User-ID and application identification are critical for granular control over network traffic.

1. **Configure User-ID**: Go to Device > User Identification and enable User-ID to map users to IP addresses.

2. **Application Control**: Navigate to Objects > Applications to enable application control based on specific applications and their characteristics.

5.3 Integrating with Other Security Solutions

1. **Cortex Integration**: Explore integrating with Cortex XSOAR for automated incident response and security orchestration.

2. **Threat Intelligence Feeds**: Consider integrating threat intelligence feeds for

enhanced threat detection.

Section 6: Conclusion

Palo Alto Networks offers a comprehensive suite of security solutions that can significantly improve an organization's cybersecurity posture. By following the steps outlined in this guide, you should now have a solid foundation for configuring, managing, and monitoring Palo Alto Networks products effectively.

Ensure you keep your device updated, audit your security policies regularly, and stay informed about new threats and best practices. As the cybersecurity landscape evolves, Palo Alto Networks remains at the forefront of innovation, providing organizations with the tools they need to protect their digital assets and maintain a secure environment.

By implementing a proactive cybersecurity strategy with Palo Alto Networks, you can minimize risks, respond effectively to threats, and safeguard your organization's critical resources.

Chapter 13: A Comprehensive Guide to Using CrowdStrike Falcon

Introduction

In today's rapidly evolving digital landscape, cybersecurity threats have become increasingly sophisticated. Organizations must adopt robust measures to protect their data and systems from potential breaches. One of the leading solutions in endpoint protection is CrowdStrike Falcon. This chapter aims to provide an in-depth guide to using CrowdStrike Falcon effectively, detailing its features, capabilities, and best practices. By the end of this guide, you will be well-equipped to utilize the CrowdStrike Falcon platform to secure your organizational environment.

1. Understanding CrowdStrike Falcon

CrowdStrike Falcon is a cloud-native endpoint protection platform that combines several cybersecurity solutions into a single product. Its primary components include:

- **Next-Generation Antivirus (NGAV):** Offers advanced malware protection using machine learning and artificial intelligence.

- **Endpoint Detection and Response (EDR):** Provides real-time monitoring and detection of suspicious activities.

- **Managed Threat Hunting:** Proactive identification of threats conducted by CrowdStrike's expert team.

- **Threat Intelligence:** Access to the latest intelligence on cyber threats and vulnerabilities.

- **IT Hygiene:** Helps maintain inventory and awareness of what's running in your environment.

1.1 Key Features

- **Lightweight Agent:** Falcon utilizes a lightweight agent installed on endpoints, which requires minimal resources and does not impact system performance.

- **Cloud-Based Architecture:** Being cloud-native, Falcon offers scalability, ease of deployment, and quick updates without the need for traditional on-premises infrastructure.

- **Real-time Visibility:** Provides organizations with real-time visibility into endpoint activities and incidents.

- **API Access:** Offers API integrations for

enhanced functionality and automation.

- **Multi-Platform Support:** Compatible with various operating systems, including Windows, macOS, and Linux.

2. Getting Started with CrowdStrike Falcon

2.1 Prerequisites

Before deploying CrowdStrike Falcon, ensure the following prerequisites are met:

- **Valid Subscription:** Obtain a valid subscription to access the CrowdStrike Falcon platform.

- **Supported Operating Systems:** Verify that your endpoints operate on supported OS versions.

- **Internet Connectivity:** Ensure that endpoints have internet access for the Falcon agent to communicate with the cloud.

2.2 Account Creation and Console Access

1. **Account Creation:**

   - Register for a CrowdStrike account through the official website. Make sure to provide accurate information for account verification.

2. **Accessing the Console:**

   - Once your account is created and verified, log in to the Falcon console using your credentials. The main dashboard will display key metrics and alert statuses.

2.3 Installing the Falcon Agent

The installation of the Falcon agent varies

depending on the operating system.

For Windows:

1. Navigate to the "Sensors" tab in the Falcon console.

2. Download the sensor installer for Windows.

3. Execute the installer on the target machine.

4. Follow the on-screen instructions, entering the necessary information, including your organization ID.

For macOS:

1. In the Falcon console, access the "Sensors" section.

2. Download the macOS sensor package.

3. Open the Terminal to install the package using the command line.

4. Follow the prompts to allow the installation and provide the organization ID.

For Linux:

1. Access the "Sensors" section of the Falcon console.

2. Download the appropriate Linux sensor package.

3. Use package management commands (like `dpkg` for Debian-based systems or `rpm` for Red Hat-based systems) to install the sensor.

4. Provide the necessary organization ID during the installation.

3. Configuring CrowdStrike Falcon Settings

After installing the agent, configuration of settings is crucial to customize the platform according to your organizational needs.

3.1 Sensor Configuration

1. **Log in to the Falcon Console:**

   - Navigate to the "Configuration" section.

2. **Selecting Sensor Settings:**

   - Review the default settings for the sensor, which include options for blocking, alerting, and reporting.

3. **Customizing Protection Modes:**

   - Adjust settings for detection and prevention modes based on your organization's risk tolerance.

4. **Defining Exclusions:**

   - Specify files, folders, or processes that

should be excluded from scanning if known to be safe.

3.2 Alert Configuration

1. **Accessing Alert Settings:**

   - In the Falcon console, navigate to "Alerts" and select "Settings."

2. **Threshold Configuration:**

   - Set thresholds for various alert types to define how sensitive the alerting mechanism should be.

3. **Notification Settings:**

   - Configure notifications to be sent to designated security personnel through email or integration with third-party services (like SIEMs).

3.3 User Roles and Permissions

1. **User Management:**

   - Navigate to the "User Management" section to define roles and permissions for users accessing the Falcon console.

2. **Role Assignment:**

   - Assign roles (e.g., Administrator, Analyst) based on the level of access each employee requires.

3. **Audit Logs:**

   - Regularly review audit logs to maintain oversight of user activities within the console.

4. Monitoring and Responding to Threats

4.1 Real-Time Monitoring

- Utilize the Falcon dashboard to gain insights into your organizational endpoints.

- Monitor active alerts and incidents to stay informed of potential threats.

- Leverage the timeline feature to review the history of actions taken on specific endpoints.

4.2 Investigating Alerts

1. **Alert Analysis:**

   - Click on individual alerts to access detailed information, including impacted hosts, timeline of the attack, and recommended actions.

2. **Utilizing Threat Intelligence:**

   - Access the integrated threat intelligence feature to gain context about the alert, including TTPs (Tactics, Techniques, and Procedures) employed by the threat actors.

3. **Conducting Enrichment:**

   - Enrich alerts with additional data by cross-referencing with your organization's existing threat intelligence frameworks.

4.3 Responding to Threats

1. **Containment:**

   - Initiate containment actions quickly through the Falcon console, which may include isolating the endpoint from the network.

2. **Remediation:**

   - Utilize the remediation tools available in Falcon to remediate files or processes flagged as malicious.

3. **Post-Incident Review:**

   - Conduct a thorough post-incident review to evaluate the effectiveness of your response and identify areas for improvement.

5. Leveraging Threat Hunting

5.1 Managed Threat Hunting Service

1. **Engaging CrowdStrike's Experts:**

   - Enlist the managed threat hunting service for proactive threat identification facilitated by CrowdStrike's expert team.

2. **Regular Reports:**

   - Receive regular reports detailing findings and recommended actions for enhancing your security posture.

5.2 Self-Directed Threat Hunting

1. **Using Search and Query Tools:**

   - Utilize built-in search capabilities and queries to hunt for indicators of compromise (IoCs) within your environment.

2. **Building Threat Scenarios:**

   - Develop threat scenarios based on your unique organizational context and simulate them to check your detection capabilities.

6. Reporting and Compliance

6.1 Generating Reports

1. **Accessing the Reporting Module:**

   - In the Falcon console, navigate to the

"Reports" section to access pre-defined report templates.

2. **Customizing Reports:**

   - Customize report parameters (such as time frames, alert types, and severity levels) to meet the needs of different stakeholders.

3. **Scheduled Reporting:**

   - Set up automated scheduled reports to be delivered to security teams and management.

6.2 Compliance Reporting

1. **Regulatory Compliance:**

   - Leverage the compliance reporting features to assist with audits for frameworks like GDPR, HIPAA, and others.

2. **Documentation:**

   - Maintain documentation detailing your security incidents and responses to provide evidence of compliance efforts.

7. Best Practices for Effective Use

7.1 Regular Training and Awareness

- Conduct regular training sessions for staff on recognizing potential threats and fortifying security protocols.

- Encourage a culture of cybersecurity awareness within your organization.

7.2 Regular Updates and Patching

- Ensure that all endpoints have the latest

security patches and updates applied to mitigate known vulnerabilities.

7.3 Continuous Improvement

- Regularly review your security policies and procedures, using insights from incident responses and threat hunting.

- Adapt your configurations in CrowdStrike Falcon based on the changing threat landscape.

CrowdStrike Falcon provides a comprehensive, cloud-native solution for endpoint protection and threat detection, equipped with powerful features and ease of use. Following the steps outlined in this chapter will enable organizations to effectively utilize Falcon for continuous monitoring, incident response, and proactive threat hunting. Ultimately, by incorporating CrowdStrike Falcon into your cybersecurity strategy, you can significantly enhance your organization's ability to combat evolving digital threats.

Chapter 14: Guide to Using Nessus

In this chapter, we will delve into the intricacies of using Nessus, one of the most prominent vulnerability scanning tools utilized in the field of cybersecurity. This guide will take you through step-by-step instructions, best practices, and strategic insights essential for effective vulnerability management using Nessus.

14.1 Introduction to Nessus

Nessus is a powerful remote security scanning tool designed to identify vulnerabilities in networked systems. It was developed by Tenable, Inc. and has gained widespread acceptance due to its comprehensive feature set. Nessus conducts passive and active network assessments, scans for missing patches, misconfigurations, and other critical vulnerabilities that may be exploited by threat actors.

215

Understanding the importance of using Nessus can be boiled down to its ability to provide a clear picture of your network's security posture, allowing organizations to take proactive measures in mitigating risks.

14.2 Setting Up Nessus

14.2.1 System Requirements

Before installing Nessus, ensure that your system meets the following requirements:

- **Operating System**: Nessus runs on various operating systems, including Windows, macOS, and various Linux distributions. Review the specific version requirements for your system.

- **Hardware Requirements**: The recommended specifications typically include at least 4GB of RAM and a dual-core processor, although more demanding scans may require additional resources.

- **Networking**: Ensure that Nessus can communicate with the target systems. This typically involves configuring firewalls and network rules.

14.2.2 Installation Steps

1. **Download Nessus:**

   - Visit the official Tenable website to download the Nessus installation package appropriate for your operating system.

2. **Run the Installer:**

   - Follow the installation prompts specific to your OS. You will generally need administrative privileges to install Nessus.

3. **Access the Web Interface:**

- After installation, Nessus can be accessed via a web browser. Navigate to `https://localhost:8834/` to launch the Nessus web interface.

4. **Configuration:**

- The initial login requires the creation of a Nessus administrator account. Follow the prompts to configure your username and strong password.

5. **Update Plugins:**

- Nessus relies on plugins to identify vulnerabilities. After logging in, head to the settings to update all plugins, ensuring you have the latest vulnerability signatures.

14.3 Navigating the Nessus Interface

Understanding the Nessus user interface is critical to effectively utilizing its features.

Here's a breakdown:

- **Dashboard**: Displays an overview of scan results, including vulnerabilities, hosts scanned, and status of previous scans.

- **Scans**: The section where you can configure and execute new scans.

  - **New Scan**: Initiate new vulnerability assessments by creating a scan template.

- **My Scans**: Displays a list of previously scheduled or completed scans with options to analyze results.

- **Vulnerabilities**: A dedicated area that displays discovered vulnerabilities sorted by severity and type.

- **Settings**: Here, you can manage user accounts, configure plugins, and other global settings.

14.4 Creating a New Scan

14.4.1 Types of Scans

Nessus offers various scan templates that cater to different requirements. Understanding each type helps in selecting the most appropriate one.

- **Basic Network Scan**: Scans specified IP addresses for vulnerabilities.

- **Web Application Tests**: Focuses on web applications, checking for SQL injection, XSS, and other web vulnerabilities.

- **Credentialed Scans**: Use valid credentials to perform an in-depth assessment of systems, yielding more accurate results.

14.4.2 Steps to Create a Scan

1. **Select Scan Type**:

   - From the "Scans" section, click on "New

Scan" and choose from the available templates.

2. **Configure the Scan Settings**:

   - **General Settings**: Name your scan and provide a description.

   - **Target Selection**: Specify the target hosts by entering IP addresses or a hostname. You can use CIDR notation to include a range of addresses.

3. **Advanced Settings (if applicable)**:

   - Configure additional settings such as scan schedule, scan options (like port scanning methods), and timeout settings.

4. **Credentials**:

   - If conducting a credentialed scan, you will input the necessary credentials for each target. This can include SSH keys for Linux systems or Windows credentials for remote service access.

5. **Save the Scan**:

   - Once all settings are configured, save the scan for immediate execution or schedule it for a later time.

14.5 Running a Scan

To run a scan, navigate to the "My Scans" section, select your newly created scan, and click "Launch". As the scan progresses, you can monitor its status and view logs to get real-time updates on the scanning process.

14.6 Analyzing Scan Results

Once a scan is complete, analyzing the results is essential to identify and prioritize vulnerabilities that require remediation.

14.6.1 Interpreting Results

1. **Vulnerability Overview**:

   - Nessus categorizes vulnerabilities into Critical, High, Moderate, and Low severity. Focus on critical and high severity first.

2. **Details Examination**:

   - Click on individual vulnerabilities to view detailed descriptions, potential impacts, solutions, and remediation steps.

3. **Exporting Results**:

   - Nessus allows you to export scan results in various formats, including PDF, CSV, and HTML. This is useful for reporting and compliance purposes.

14.7 Remediation and Best Practices

223

After identifying vulnerabilities, the next critical step is remediation. Here are best practices to follow:

14.7.1 Prioritize Vulnerabilities:

- Use the severity scoring to prioritize which vulnerabilities to address first.

- Consider the business impact of the affected systems when prioritizing.

14.7.2 Mitigation Strategies:

- Patch management should be a routine procedure to fix identified vulnerabilities promptly.

- Ensure misconfigurations are remediated by applying security best practices.

14.7.3 Continuous Monitoring:

- Regularly schedule scans to continuously

monitor your environment for new vulnerabilities that may arise.

14.7.4 Training and Awareness:

- Ensure that your team is well-versed in the use of Nessus through training sessions. Keeping up on vulnerability management best practices is crucial for long-term success.

14.8 Advanced Features of Nessus

Nessus is not just a basic vulnerability scanner; it offers advanced functionalities too.

14.8.1 Compliance Checks:

- Nessus can perform compliance checks against various standards and regulations like PCI-DSS or HIPAA, offering insights into compliance status.

14.8.2 Policy Management:

- Create and manage scan policies to ensure consistent scanning tactics across environments.

14.8.3 Integrations:

- Integrate Nessus with other security tools and SIEM systems for enhanced visibility and incident response.

14.9 Troubleshooting and Support

While scanning and remediation processes flow smoothly most of the time, there might be instances where issues arise.

14.9.1 Common Issues and Solutions:

- **Incomplete Scans**: Ensure that the targets are reachable and that there are no firewall restrictions blocking Nessus.

- **Plugin Failures**: Update plugins regularly to ensure compatibility and access the latest vulnerability checks.

14.9.2 Accessing Support:

- Tenable offers comprehensive documentation and community forums for troubleshooting and user support. In addition, consider professional services for more complex environments.

14.10 Conclusion

Nessus is a critical tool for security professionals looking to enhance their organizations' security posture. By following this step-by-step guide, cybersecurity practitioners can leverage Nessus effectively to identify, prioritize, and remediate vulnerabilities, ensuring a robust security posture against emerging threats. Remember, the landscape of cybersecurity is constantly evolving, and maintaining an updated and proactive vulnerability management program with tools such as Nessus is essential for safeguarding sensitive data and systems.

Chapter 15: A Guide to Using Cyber Threat Intelligence Tools: Collection, Analysis, and Sharing of Threat Information

In the ever-evolving landscape of cybersecurity, the reliance on Cyber Threat Intelligence (CTI) tools is paramount for organizations aiming to protect their digital assets. This chapter will guide you step-by-step through the process of leveraging CTI tools for the effective collection, analysis, and sharing of threat information.

Introduction to Cyber Threat Intelligence

Cyber Threat Intelligence refers to the knowledge and understanding of threats that can help organizations defend against cyber attacks. It encompasses the collection, analysis, and dissemination of actionable information about potential or existing threats. By effectively using CTI tools, organizations can bolster their security posture, improve incident response times, and achieve better overall cybersecurity.

Step 1: Understanding Your Organization's Needs

Before diving into the specifics of CTI tools, it is crucial to assess your organization's needs:

1. **Identify Objectives**: Understand what you aim to achieve with CTI. Do you want to proactively identify threats, enhance incident response, or comply with regulations?

2. **Define Scope**: Determine the scope of your threat intelligence needs. Are you focusing on specific industries, geographical areas, or types of threats (like ransomware, DDoS attacks, etc.)?

3. **Involve Stakeholders**: Engage various departments, including IT, security, risk management, and compliance, to gather insights on their CTI requirements.

Step 2: Collecting Threat Intelligence

Collection is the first and foremost stage of leveraging CTI. Here are the key methods and tools for effective threat data collection:

2.1. Threat Intelligence Platforms (TIPs)

TIPs aggregate and normalize threat data from various sources. Popular TIPs include:

- **MISP (Malware Information Sharing Platform)**: MISP allows organizations to share structured threat information efficiently. It supports information collection, storage, and sharing among a community of users.

- **ThreatConnect**: This platform provides not just threat collection but also the tools necessary for analysis and operationalization.

2.2. Open Source Intelligence (OSINT)

OSINT tools facilitate the gathering of publicly available information. Consider using:

- **Shodan**: Shodan is a search engine for internet-connected devices. By using filters, you can discover vulnerable infrastructure susceptible to attacks.

- **VirusTotal**: It aggregates multiple antivirus engines to analyze files and URLs for malware. This can assist in identifying malicious IPs or domains.

2.3. Commercial Threat Feeds

Engage providers of commercial threat feeds that supply real-time data on threats, vulnerabilities, and exploits. Some well-known providers include:

- **CrowdStrike**: Offers an extensive repository of threat intelligence data based on their global experience in combating cyberattacks.

- **Recorded Future**: Provides insights into threats and vulnerabilities through a combination of machine learning and human analysis.

2.4. Community Sharing

Join forums, communities, and organizations that share threat intelligence. Platforms like:

- **AlienVault Open Threat Exchange (OTX)**: A collaborative platform to share actionable threat intelligence with peers.

- **ISACs (Information Sharing and Analysis Centers)**: These sector-specific organizations share threat data and foster collaboration among members.

Step 3: Analyzing Collected Data

Once data is collected, the next step involves analyzing it to produce actionable insights. Effective analysis relies on certain techniques and tools:

3.1. Data Normalization and Enrichment

Data coming from various sources may have

different structures. Leverage tools for:

- **Normalization**: Transforming data into a common format to streamline analysis. Tools like MISP can help normalize various threat data sets.

- **Enrichment**: Adding context to the collected data to help establish the severity and relevance of the threats. For this, consider using:

  - **Threat intelligence enrich services**: Such as ThreatCrowd or IPinfo, which provide detailed information about IP addresses, URLs, or domains.

3.2. Threat Analysis Frameworks

Utilizing established frameworks helps analyze the threat landscape effectively.

Frameworks such as:

- **MITRE ATT&CK**: Provides a matrix of known adversary tactics and techniques that can be used to identify and counteract threats.

- **Diamond Model of Intrusion Analysis**: A structured approach to analyzing adversary actions, capabilities, and targets can facilitate a clearer understanding of attack patterns.

3.3. Use of Analytics Tools

Incorporate analytics tools to visualize and understand connections between threats. Tools like:

- **Maltego**: A powerful data mining tool that visualizes relationships among different entities (e.g., IPs, domains).

- **Data loss prevention (DLP)** solutions: Focused on analyzing the flow of sensitive information and identifying potential risks associated with its leakage.

3.4. Produce Intelligence Reports

Create intelligence reports that summarize your findings and insights from the analysis. Follow these guidelines:

1. **Executive Summary**: Provide key insights for decision-makers.

2. **Detailed Analysis**: Include methodology, data sources, findings, and recommendations.

3. **Infographics**: Use visuals to simplify complex data for easier consumption.

Step 4: Sharing Threat Intelligence

After analysis, it's crucial to share pivotal threat intelligence with relevant internal and external stakeholders while ensuring compliance with data privacy regulations.

4.1. Internal Sharing

Disseminate threat intelligence across the organization to enhance awareness and prepare for potential threats:

- **Create a CTI Portal**: Facilitate easy access for all teams to review threat intelligence findings.

- **Team Briefings**: Conduct regular briefings or training sessions to update staff on significant threats or trends observed.

4.2. External Sharing

Engage in responsible sharing with trusted partners and industry organizations. Here are some methods to consider:

- **Threat Sharing Communities**: Such as OTX or ISACs, can help establish trust and facilitate data sharing. This enables organizations to benefit from collective knowledge.

- **Shared Reporting Systems**: Implement reporting mechanisms based on platforms like MISP, allowing organizations to report and track threats collectively.

4.3. Adhering to Compliance and Regulations

Ensure that the sharing of threat intelligence adheres to local and international regulations, such as GDPR. Consider:

- **Anonymization**: Remove any personally identifiable information (PII) before sharing threat data.

- **Clear Policies**: Document and communicate the policies for data sharing to all stakeholders to ensure compliance.

Step 5: Continuous Improvement

Cyber Threat Intelligence is not a one-time initiative but an ongoing process. As the threat landscape evolves, so should your approach:

5.1. Review and Update

Regularly review your CTI processes, tools, and methodologies:

- **Post-Incident Reviews**: Analyze past incidents to modify CTI strategies and ensure they are effective in real-world scenarios.

- **Tool and Data Source Assessment**: Periodically evaluate if your CTI tools meet your organization's changing needs and if they provide relevant and up-to-date threat intelligence.

5.2. Training and Skill Development

Invest in continuous training for your cybersecurity team:

- **Workshops and Seminars**: Leverage external resources to stay informed on the latest CTI trends and tools.

- **Certifications**: Encourage professionals on your team to achieve relevant certifications (e.g., Certified Threat Intelligence Analyst - CTIA) to bolster their skills.

5.3. Stay Informed of Emerging Threats

Follow cybersecurity news, subscribe to relevant threat intelligence feeds, and participate in industry webinars hosted by cybersecurity leaders to stay ahead of emerging threats.

Effective use of Cyber Threat Intelligence tools can profoundly impact your organization's cybersecurity strategy. By following the steps outlined in this chapter, you will not only be equipped to collect and analyze threat data but also enhance your organization's resilience against cyber threats through informed threat intelligence sharing.

Continual improvement and a proactive stance will ensure your organization remains agile in a landscape rife with evolving cyber risks.

Chapter 15: A Guide to Using Cyber Threat Intelligence Tools: Collection, Analysis, and Sharing of Threat Information

In the ever-evolving landscape of cybersecurity, the reliance on Cyber Threat Intelligence (CTI) tools is paramount for organizations aiming to protect their digital assets. This chapter will guide you step-by-step through the process of leveraging CTI tools for the effective collection, analysis, and sharing of threat information.

Introduction to Cyber Threat Intelligence

Cyber Threat Intelligence refers to the knowledge and understanding of threats that can help organizations defend against cyber attacks. It encompasses the collection, analysis, and dissemination of actionable information about potential or existing threats. By effectively using CTI tools, organizations can bolster their security posture, improve incident response times, and achieve better overall cybersecurity.

Step 1: Understanding Your Organization's Needs

Before diving into the specifics of CTI tools, it is crucial to assess your organization's needs:

1. **Identify Objectives**: Understand what you aim to achieve with CTI. Do you want to proactively identify threats, enhance incident response, or comply with regulations?

2. **Define Scope**: Determine the scope of your threat intelligence needs. Are you focusing on specific industries, geographical areas, or types of threats (like ransomware, DDoS attacks, etc.)?

3. **Involve Stakeholders**: Engage various departments, including IT, security, risk management, and compliance, to gather insights on their CTI requirements.

Step 2: Collecting Threat Intelligence

Collection is the first and foremost stage of leveraging CTI. Here are the key methods and tools for effective threat data collection:

2.1. Threat Intelligence Platforms (TIPs)

TIPs aggregate and normalize threat data from various sources. Popular TIPs include:

- **MISP (Malware Information Sharing Platform)**: MISP allows organizations to share structured threat information efficiently.

It supports information collection, storage, and sharing among a community of users.

- **ThreatConnect**: This platform provides not just threat collection but also the tools necessary for analysis and operationalization.

2.2. Open Source Intelligence (OSINT)

OSINT tools facilitate the gathering of publicly available information. Consider using:

- **Shodan**: Shodan is a search engine for internet-connected devices. By using filters, you can discover vulnerable infrastructure susceptible to attacks.

- **VirusTotal**: It aggregates multiple antivirus engines to analyze files and URLs for malware. This can assist in identifying malicious IPs or domains.

2.3. Commercial Threat Feeds

Engage providers of commercial threat feeds that supply real-time data on threats, vulnerabilities, and exploits. Some well-known providers include:

- **CrowdStrike**: Offers an extensive repository of threat intelligence data based on their global experience in combating cyberattacks.

- **Recorded Future**: Provides insights into threats and vulnerabilities through a combination of machine learning and human analysis.

2.4. Community Sharing

Join forums, communities, and organizations that share threat intelligence. Platforms like:

- **AlienVault Open Threat Exchange (OTX)**: A collaborative platform to share actionable threat intelligence with peers.

- **ISACs (Information Sharing and Analysis Centers)**: These sector-specific organizations share threat data and foster collaboration among members.

Step 3: Analyzing Collected Data

Once data is collected, the next step involves analyzing it to produce actionable insights. Effective analysis relies on certain techniques and tools:

3.1. Data Normalization and Enrichment

Data coming from various sources may have different structures. Leverage tools for:

- **Normalization**: Transforming data into a common format to streamline analysis. Tools like MISP can help normalize various threat data sets.

- **Enrichment**: Adding context to the collected data to help establish the severity and relevance of the threats. For this, consider using:

  - **Threat intelligence enrich services**: Such as ThreatCrowd or IPinfo, which provide detailed information about IP addresses, URLs, or domains.

3.2. Threat Analysis Frameworks

Utilizing established frameworks helps

analyze the threat landscape effectively. Frameworks such as:

- **MITRE ATT&CK**: Provides a matrix of known adversary tactics and techniques that can be used to identify and counteract threats.

- **Diamond Model of Intrusion Analysis**: A structured approach to analyzing adversary actions, capabilities, and targets can facilitate a clearer understanding of attack patterns.

3.3. Use of Analytics Tools

Incorporate analytics tools to visualize and understand connections between threats. Tools like:

- **Maltego**: A powerful data mining tool that visualizes relationships among different entities (e.g., IPs, domains).

- **Data loss prevention (DLP)** solutions: Focused on analyzing the flow of sensitive information and identifying potential risks associated with its leakage.

3.4. Produce Intelligence Reports

Create intelligence reports that summarize your findings and insights from the analysis. Follow these guidelines:

1. **Executive Summary**: Provide key insights for decision-makers.

2. **Detailed Analysis**: Include methodology, data sources, findings, and recommendations.

3. **Infographics**: Use visuals to simplify complex data for easier consumption.

Step 4: Sharing Threat Intelligence

After analysis, it's crucial to share pivotal threat intelligence with relevant internal and external stakeholders while ensuring compliance with data privacy regulations.

4.1. Internal Sharing

Disseminate threat intelligence across the organization to enhance awareness and prepare for potential threats:

- **Create a CTI Portal**: Facilitate easy access for all teams to review threat intelligence findings.

- **Team Briefings**: Conduct regular briefings or training sessions to update staff on significant threats or trends observed.

4.2. External Sharing

Engage in responsible sharing with trusted partners and industry organizations. Here are some methods to consider:

- **Threat Sharing Communities**: Such as OTX or ISACs, can help establish trust and facilitate data sharing. This enables organizations to benefit from collective knowledge.

- **Shared Reporting Systems**: Implement reporting mechanisms based on platforms like MISP, allowing organizations to report and track threats collectively.

4.3. Adhering to Compliance and Regulations

Ensure that the sharing of threat intelligence adheres to local and international regulations, such as GDPR. Consider:

- **Anonymization**: Remove any personally identifiable information (PII) before sharing threat data.

- **Clear Policies**: Document and communicate the policies for data sharing to all stakeholders to ensure compliance.

Step 5: Continuous Improvement

Cyber Threat Intelligence is not a one-time initiative but an ongoing process. As the threat landscape evolves, so should your approach:

5.1. Review and Update

Regularly review your CTI processes, tools, and methodologies:

- **Post-Incident Reviews**: Analyze past incidents to modify CTI strategies and ensure they are effective in real-world scenarios.

- **Tool and Data Source Assessment**: Periodically evaluate if your CTI tools meet your organization's changing needs and if they provide relevant and up-to-date threat intelligence.

5.2. Training and Skill Development

Invest in continuous training for your cybersecurity team:

- **Workshops and Seminars**: Leverage external resources to stay informed on the latest CTI trends and tools.

- **Certifications**: Encourage professionals on your team to achieve relevant certifications (e.g., Certified Threat Intelligence Analyst - CTIA) to bolster their skills.

5.3. Stay Informed of Emerging Threats

Follow cybersecurity news, subscribe to relevant threat intelligence feeds, and participate in industry webinars hosted by cybersecurity leaders to stay ahead of emerging threats.

Effective use of Cyber Threat Intelligence tools can profoundly impact your organization's cybersecurity strategy. By following the steps outlined in this chapter, you will not only be equipped to collect and analyze threat data but also enhance your organization's resilience against cyber threats through informed threat intelligence sharing. Continual improvement and a proactive stance will ensure your organization remains agile in a landscape rife with evolving cyber risks.

Chapter 16: Complete Guide to Using Cisco Email Security

Introduction

Cisco Email Security is a comprehensive solution designed to protect organizations from a variety of email-based threats such as spam, phishing, malware, and other malicious attacks. This guide aims to provide a step-by-step overview of how to effectively use Cisco Email Security, detailing setup, configuration, management, and troubleshooting processes.

1. Understanding Cisco Email Security

1.1 What is Cisco Email Security?

Cisco Email Security is an appliance or cloud-based service that secures email communications through a range of features:

spam filtering, malware detection, data loss prevention (DLP), encryption, and advanced threat protection. It helps prevent unauthorized access to sensitive information while ensuring the integrity of email communications.

1.2 Key Features

- **Spam Filtering**: Identifying and blocking unwanted emails.

- **Malware Protection**: Scanning incoming emails for harmful attachments.

- **Phishing Detection**: Recognizing and mitigating phishing attempts.

- **Data Loss Prevention**: Preventing sensitive data from being sent outside the organization.

- **Encryption**: Securing email content via encryption during transmission.

- **Reporting and Analytics**: Providing

insights through detailed reports and dashboards.

2. Getting Started with Cisco Email Security

2.1 Prerequisites

Before deploying Cisco Email Security, ensure that you have:

- A valid license for Cisco Email Security.

- Access to the Cisco Email Security appliance or web portal.

- Basic knowledge of email systems and network configuration.

2.2 Deployment Options

Cisco Email Security can be deployed in different ways:

- **Physical Appliance**: Hardware device installed on-premises.

- **Virtual Appliance**: Software version that runs on virtualization platforms.

- **Cloud-Based Solution**: Cisco Cloud Email Security which requires no on-premises hardware.

2.3 Installation

Step 1: Choose Deployment Type

- Decide whether you are using a physical, virtual, or cloud-based version based on your organization's needs.

Step 2: Download the Software

- For virtual appliances, download the ISO file

from the Cisco website.

Step 3: Follow Installation Procedures

- For physical and virtual installations, follow the hardware/user manual included with the appliance.

3. Initial Configuration

3.1 Accessing the Management Console

Step 1: Connect to the network

- Ensure the device is connected to the appropriate network segment (management network).

Step 2: Access via Web Browser

- Open a web browser and enter the management IP address of your appliance.

263

Step 3: Log in

- Use the default administrative credentials to log into the management console.

3.2 Setting Up Basic Settings

Step 1: Change Default Password

- Navigate to the Account Management section and change the default password.

Step 2: Configure Networking

- Go to the Network Configuration settings to set up IP address, gateway, DNS servers, etc.

Step 3: Set Time and Time Zone

- It's crucial to set the correct time zone for logging and reporting.

3.3 Domain Configuration

Step 1: Add Your Domain

- In the email settings area, proceed to add your organization's domain(s) that will be protected.

Step 2: Configure MX Records

- Update the DNS MX records to point to your Cisco Email Security appliance.

Step 3: Verify Configuration

- Use tools like `dig` or `nslookup` to ensure DNS changes have propagated correctly.

4. Advanced Configuration

4.1 Email Policies

Step 1: Access Policies Configuration

- Go to the "Mail Policies" section in the dashboard.

Step 2: Create Spam Policies

- Set filters for spam detection, including threshold levels and actions to take on suspected spam.

Step 3: Set Malware Scanning Policies

- Configure real-time scanning options and choose how to deal with detected malware.

4.2 Data Loss Prevention (DLP)

Step 1: Define DLP Policies

- Determine what constitutes sensitive information within your organization.

Step 2: Configure Actions

- Set what actions should be taken when sensitive data is detected in outgoing emails.

4.3 User and Group Management

Step 1: Add Users

- Navigate to the User Management section to manually add users or sync with an existing directory service.

Step 2: Create Groups

- Organize users into groups for easier policy management.

4.4 Reporting and Logs

Step 1: Access Reporting Interface

- Go to the "Reports" section to view predefined reports.

Step 2: Customize Reports

- Create custom reports based on criteria relevant to your organization's needs.

5. Maintenance and Management

5.1 Regular Updates

Step 1: Check for Updates

- Regularly check the Cisco website for updates or patches.

Step 2: Schedule Updates

- Configure auto-updates to keep the appliance running the latest software.

5.2 Backups

Step 1: Regular Backups

- Use the Backup section to create backups of your configuration settings.

Step 2: Store Backups Securely

- Ensure that backups are stored in a secure location to prevent unauthorized access.

5.3 Monitoring Performance

Step 1: Set Alerts

- Configure alerts for system performance and email traffic anomalies.

Step 2: Analyze Logs

- Regularly review logs to identify any potential security incidents or system issues.

6. Troubleshooting Common Issues

6.1 Email Delivery Problems

Step 1: Check Bounce Messages

- Review bounce-back messages for clues.

Step 2: Analyze Logs

- Use the logging feature to trace issues in email routing or delivery.

6.2 User Access Issues

Step 1: Check User Permissions

- Verify that users have the necessary permissions to access the system.

Step 2: Reset Passwords

- For users having trouble logging in, reset

their passwords by using the account management feature.

Conclusion

Cisco Email Security is a robust solution that can greatly enhance your organization's email security posture. By following the steps outlined in this guide, you can effectively deploy, configure, manage, and troubleshoot your Cisco Email Security installation. Continuous monitoring and updating are essential to adapting to evolving email threats, ensuring the safety of your organization's communications.

Chapter 17: A Comprehensive Guide to Using Symantec Data Loss Prevention (DLP)

Introduction to Symantec DLP

Data Loss Prevention (DLP) is an essential component in an organization's cybersecurity strategy. Synonymous with the protection of sensitive data, DLP solutions such as Symantec DLP help prevent unauthorized access and data leaks, ensuring compliance with regulations like GDPR and HIPAA. This chapter will walk you through the installation, configuration, and management of Symantec DLP, detailing every step to ensure a comprehensive understanding and effective deployment of this critical tool.

Section 1: Understanding the Key Components of Symantec DLP

Before diving into installation, it's essential to understand the key components of Symantec DLP:

- **Endpoint Agents**: Installed on user devices to monitor and protect sensitive data at rest, in use, and in motion.

- **Network Prevention**: Monitors network traffic to identify and block unauthorized data transmissions.

- **Storage**: Protects sensitive data stored in file repositories, databases, and cloud storage services.

- **Console**: A centralized management interface for configuring policies, generating reports, and monitoring incidents.

- **Reporting and Dashboard**: Provides

insights into data protection efforts, incidents, and overall compliance posture.

Understanding these components helps in effectively utilizing Symantec DLP and implementing a comprehensive data protection strategy tailored to your organization's needs.

Section 2: Installation of Symantec DLP

Step 1: Preparing for Installation

1. **System Requirements**: Review the hardware and software requirements for Symantec DLP. Ensure that the server hosting DLP complies with these requirements, including adequate CPU, RAM, and storage capacities.

2. **Licensing**: Obtain the appropriate

licenses for Symantec DLP. Licensing may vary based on the number of endpoints and functionalities required.

3. **Pre-Installation Checks**: Disable any conflicting software, and ensure that the server is updated with the latest patches and updates.

Step 2: Downloading the Software

1. Access the Symantec website or the relevant vendor portal.

2. Navigate to the downloads section and select the appropriate version of Symantec DLP.

3. Download the installation package, which should include all necessary components for installation.

Step 3: Installing the Software

1. **Run the Installer**: Launch the installation wizard. You may need administrative privileges to proceed.

2. **Follow the Prompts**: Accept the license agreement and select the components to install. Generally, it's advisable to install the full suite unless you have a specific requirement.

3. **Enter Configuration Details**: Configure the database settings. You may choose between using an embedded database or an existing SQL server.

4. **Complete Installation**: Review your installation choices and complete the setup. Restart the server if prompted.

Section 3: Configuring Symantec DLP

After installation, you will need to configure Symantec DLP to align with your organization's data protection policies.

Step 1: Accessing the Console

1. **Login**: Open a web browser and navigate to the console URL. Enter your administrative credentials to access the management interface.

Step 2: Setting Up Policies

1. **Navigate to Policy Management**: Find the policy management section within the console.

2. **Create a New Policy**: Click on the "Create Policy" button. You will be presented

with a series of templates to choose from.

3. **Select a Template**: Choose a template relevant to your organizational needs—this could include specific industry regulations or general data protection.

4. **Define Rule Conditions**: Specify the conditions that will trigger the policy. For example, if the data contains Social Security Numbers, or if it is transmitted outside the corporate network.

5. **Configure Actions**: Determine what actions should be applied when violations occur, such as blocking the transmission, alerting an administrator, or encrypting the data.

6. **Testing the Policy**: Before deploying widely, use a test group to evaluate the effectiveness of the policy.

Step 3: Deploying Endpoint Agents

1. **Preparing Endpoint Deployment**: Gather all endpoints that require protection.

2. **Choose Deployment Method**: Decide between manual installation, push deployment through Group Policy, or other deployment tools.

3. **Install Endpoint Agent**: Follow the specific steps based on the chosen method to install the Symantec DLP endpoint agent on user devices.

4. **Configuration of Endpoint Policies**: Align endpoint agent settings with the overarching DLP policies you have created.

Section 4: Incident Management

The primary purpose of DLP solutions is to manage incidents effectively as they arise.

Step 1: Monitoring Incidents

1. **Dashboard Overview**: Use the dashboard to get a high-level overview of incidents in real-time.

2. **Drill Down into Incidents**: Click on specific incidents to investigate further. Review details like the nature of the violation, data involved, and user actions.

Step 2: Responding to Incidents

1. **Evaluate the Incident**: Determine the severity and the potential impact of each incident.

2. **Take Action**: Depending on the severity, you may choose to escalate the incident, take corrective action, or implement additional preventive measures.

3. **Document Actions Taken**: Maintain records of each incident and the response for auditing and compliance purposes.

Section 5: Reporting and Compliance

Step 1: Generating Reports

1. **Navigate to the Reporting Section**: Access the reporting tools within the Symantec DLP console.

2. **Select Report Types**: Choose between different reporting options—incident reports, compliance reports, and policy effectiveness reports.

3. **Schedule Automated Reports**: Consider setting up automated reports on a daily, weekly, or monthly basis to keep stakeholders informed.

Step 2: Ensuring Compliance

1. **Review Compliance Needs**: Understand the regulatory requirements your organization must adhere to.

2. **Align DLP Policies**: Ensure that the DLP policies you've set are in compliance with industry regulations.

3. **Audit and Adjust**: Regularly audit your DLP policies and adjust them based on compliance needs and operational changes within your organization.

Section 6: Best Practices for Using Symantec DLP

1. **User Training**: Conduct regular training sessions for employees to increase awareness regarding data protection policies and the role of DLP.

2. **Continuous Monitoring**: Regularly monitor the system for potential vulnerabilities and policy effectiveness.

3. **Review and Adjust Policies**: DLP is not a set-and-forget solution. Regularly review and adjust your policies to adapt to new threats and changes within your organization.

4. **Incident Review**: After any incident has been handled, conduct a post-event analysis to determine improvements or changes needed in your policies or responses.

5. **Stay Informed**: Continually update your knowledge about new features, security threats, and compliance regulations affecting your industry.

Implementing and effectively managing Symantec DLP requires a clear understanding of its components, careful planning of installation and configuration, vigilant incident management, and ongoing reporting to ensure compliance. By following this comprehensive guide step by step, your organization can effectively protect sensitive data, manage potential incidents, and comply with various regulatory requirements. Embrace the evolving landscape of data protection with Symantec DLP – it's a fundamental step toward securing your organization's most valuable asset: its data.

Chapter 18: A Comprehensive Guide to Using EnCase

Introduction

In the realm of digital forensics, EnCase has positioned itself as one of the leading software solutions used for data recovery, evidence gathering, and digital investigation. Its robust features and reliable performance make it a favorite among law enforcement agencies, corporate security teams, and forensic investigators alike. In this chapter, we will delve into the details of using EnCase, breaking it down into various steps and components for ease of understanding.

What is EnCase?

EnCase is a digital forensic software suite developed by Guidance Software (now part of OpenText). It allows forensic investigators to examine hard drives, mobile devices, cloud data, and other digital evidence in a forensically sound manner. The software enables users to capture, analyze, and report on digital evidence while maintaining the integrity of the data.

Key Features of EnCase

Before diving into the step-by-step guide, it is essential to understand some of the critical features of EnCase:

1. **Data Acquisition**: EnCase allows for the creation of forensic images of storage devices, ensuring that data can be analyzed without altering the original evidence.

2. **File System Analysis**: The software can parse file systems and recover deleted files, providing a comprehensive overview of the data stored on a device.

3. **Keyword Searches**: Investigators can perform advanced keyword searches across entire datasets to pinpoint relevant information based on search terms.

4. **Timeline Analysis**: EnCase can create timelines of file activity and usage, helping investigators understand the sequence of events leading up to an incident.

5. **Reporting Tools**: The software includes powerful reporting capabilities, allowing users to generate detailed reports of their findings.

6. **Scriptability**: EnCase supports scripting, enabling users to automate repetitive tasks and create customized workflows.

7. **Integration with Other Tools**: EnCase can be used alongside other forensic tools, enhancing the overall capabilities of an

investigation.

Step-by-Step Guide to Using EnCase

Step 1: Preparing for Investigation

1.1 Gathering Equipment

Before beginning your investigation, ensure you have all the necessary equipment:

- A computer running EnCase.

- Write blockers to prevent changes to the evidence during acquisition.

- External storage devices for data transfer.

- Specific hardware for cell phone extraction if needed.

1.2 Documenting the Scene

Document the physical scene where the digital evidence is located. This may include taking photographs, noting the condition of devices, and listing serial numbers. Proper documentation is crucial for maintaining a chain of custody.

Step 2: Acquiring Data

2.1 Connecting Devices

Once on-site, connect the target storage device to your forensic workstation. If it's a computer hard drive, use a write blocker to prevent any data modification during the imaging process.

2.2 Creating Forensic Images

- **Open EnCase**: Start EnCase on your

forensic workstation.

- **Select "Create Image"**: In the main interface, choose the option to create a forensic image. This is typically found in the "File" or "Evidence" menu.

- **Choose the Source Device**: Select the connected storage device from the list presented by EnCase.

- **Select Imaging Options**: Choose the type of imaging (e.g., raw dd image, E01 image, etc.) and any additional options, such as verifying the image upon completion.

- **Name and Save the Image File**: Provide a file name and specify the location on your external storage where the image will be saved.

- **Start the Imaging Process**: Begin the imaging process and monitor its progress. Depending on the size of the device, this could take a significant amount of time.

2.3 Verifying Integrity

Once the imaging process is complete, EnCase will generate a hash value for both the source device and the forensic image. Verify that these hashes match to ensure the integrity of the data.

Step 3: Analyzing the Data

3.1 Importing Forensic Images

- **Open the Forensic Image**: In EnCase, you can create a new case or open an existing case. Select "Add Evidence" to import the forensic image you created.

- **Examine the File System**: Once the image is loaded, EnCase will display the file system structure. You can explore folders and files similar to traditional file exploration.

3.2 Recovering Deleted Files

- **Use File Carving Techniques**: EnCase allows users to apply file carving techniques to recover deleted files. Navigate to the "Search" or "File" menus and select the option for recovering deleted items.

- **Filter and Sort Results**: Use filters to narrow down your search based on file types, dates, or other criteria.

3.3 Performing Keyword Searches

- **Keyword Search Functionality**: Access the keyword search option within EnCase.

Enter the specific terms you wish to search for and initiate the search across the evidence files.

- **Refining Searches**: Utilize Boolean operators (AND, OR, NOT) to refine your search results further, making it easier to pinpoint critical evidence.

Step 4: Timeline Analysis

4.1 Creating a Timeline

- **Select the Timeline Tool**: From the EnCase menu, navigate to the timeline analysis feature.

- **Choose Events to Include**: Select the types of events you want to track, such as file creation, modification, and access times.

- **Generate the Timeline**: Allow EnCase to process the information, generating a visual timeline of the events associated with the data in your evidence.

4.2 Analyzing Event Correlation

- **Examine Event Relationships**: Use the timeline to correlate activities and better understand the sequence of actions taken on the device.

Step 5: Reporting Findings:

5.1 Generating Reports

- **Access the Reporting Module**: Navigate to the reporting section of EnCase.

- **Select Information to Include**: Choose

the findings, events, or sections of the investigation that you wish to report on.

- **Customize the Report**: Utilize available templates in EnCase, or create a custom report format that meets the requirements for your audience (law enforcement, legal teams, etc.).

- **Export and Save the Report**: Once the report is generated, save it in the desired format (e.g., PDF, HTML, etc.) for sharing and documentation.

5.2 Presenting Evidence

- **Preparing for Court**: If your findings are to be used in a court case, ensure the report adheres to the appropriate standards. Be prepared to present your findings clearly and concisely.

Step 6: Best Practices and Ethical Considerations

6.1 Adhering to Standard Protocols

Always follow established forensic protocols and standards, such as those set by the International Organization on Computer Evidence (IOCE) or guidelines from your organization. This includes maintaining a strict chain of custody and ensuring that all actions taken during the investigation can be replicated.

6.2 Ethical Considerations

Maintain ethical boundaries during your investigation. This entails respecting privacy rights, not exceeding the scope of your investigation, and ensuring that all evidence is handled with care.

Conclusion

EnCase is a powerful tool for digital forensic investigations. By following the appropriate steps and best practices outlined in this guide, forensic investigators can leverage EnCase to uncover valuable digital evidence while ensuring the integrity and security of the data. Whether you are a seasoned professional or a newcomer to digital forensics, mastering EnCase can significantly enhance your investigative capabilities. The information gleaned from digital investigations not only serves to support legal cases but also to enhance overall cybersecurity measures and protocols within organizations. Remember, the key to successful digital forensics lies not just in the tools you use but in your understanding of the processes and methodologies that underpin thorough investigations.

Chapter 19: Training and Professional Development for SOC Analysts

The need for skilled professionals in the realm of cybersecurity has never been greater. As organizations increasingly rely on technological solutions to streamline operations and store sensitive data, the potential for cyber threats grows exponentially. Security Operations Center (SOC) analysts play a pivotal role in defending these infrastructures from myriad cyber attacks. This chapter delves into the essential aspects of training and professional development for SOC analysts, components that are crucial for maintaining an effective security posture in any organization.

19.1 The Role of SOC Analysts

Before discussing the training and development pertinent to SOC analysts, it's essential to define their role within an organization:

- **Incident Detection and Response**: SOC analysts are tasked with monitoring security alerts, analyzing incidents, and responding to threats. They utilize various security information and event management (SIEM) tools to detect anomalous behaviors and potential threats in the network.

- **Threat Hunting**: In addition to reactive measures, SOC analysts actively search for vulnerabilities and threats within the infrastructure, often before they manifest as issues.

- **Forensics and Investigation**: In the aftermath of a security incident, SOC analysts conduct investigations to identify the source and impact of the breach. This involves collecting evidence, analyzing data, and escalating findings to higher-level cybersecurity teams.

- **Reporting**: Effective communication of findings and actions taken is a critical part of the SOC analyst's responsibilities. Preparing detailed reports for management and stakeholders regarding security incidents and operational metrics is essential for organizational awareness.

Given the complexity and ever-evolving nature of cyber threats, SOC analysts must undergo continual training and professional development to keep abreast of the latest tools, techniques, and methods employed by cybercriminals.

19.2 Foundations of SOC Analyst Training

Training for SOC analysts can be categorized into foundational training, ongoing education, specialization, and certification.

19.2.1 Foundational Training

New analysts often begin their journey by building a solid foundation in cybersecurity principles. This may involve:

- **Understanding Cybersecurity Basics**: This includes learning about the CIA triad (Confidentiality, Integrity, Availability) and various types of cyber threats, such as malware, phishing, and denial-of-service attacks.

- **Networking and System Administration**: A robust understanding of networking concepts, operating systems (particularly UNIX/Linux and Windows environments), and systems administration is crucial. Analysts should know how networks operate, protocols used, and how to manage and secure servers.

- **Security Tools Training**: Familiarity with tools such as firewalls, intrusion detection systems (IDS), intrusion prevention systems (IPS), and SIEM solutions is fundamental. Analysts should undergo hands-on training with these tools to understand their configurations, capabilities, and limitations.

19.2.2 Ongoing Education

Given the rapid pace of technological change, ongoing education is vital for SOC analysts. This education can take various forms:

- **Workshops and Webinars**: Participating in relevant workshops and webinars can provide SOC analysts with updates on recent threats and new tools or strategies being employed in the industry.

- **Online Courses**: There are various platforms offering courses on specific technologies or approaches in cybersecurity. Platforms like Cybrary, Coursera, and Udemy can be excellent places for analysts to broaden their expertise.

- **Industry Conferences**: Attending cybersecurity conferences such as RSA, Black Hat, or DEF CON offers SOC analysts exposure to the latest trends, techniques, and tools in the field. Networking with peers and industry leaders provides insights that can be directly applied to their work.

19.2.3 Specialization

Once SOC analysts have obtained foundational knowledge and engaged in ongoing education, many choose to specialize in specific areas of cybersecurity. Some common specializations among SOC analysts include:

- **Incident Response**: This specialization focuses on protocols and practices for responding to security incidents, from initial detection through to forensic analysis and recovery.

- **Threat Intelligence**: Analysts specializing in threat intelligence monitor and analyze threat data to anticipate potential attacks. They focus on understanding attacker methodologies, tactics, techniques, and procedures (TTPs).

- **Compliance and Risk Management**: In this area, analysts ensure organizational compliance with various cybersecurity regulations (such as GDPR or HIPAA) while working on risk assessments to identify and mitigate potential vulnerabilities.

19.2.4 Certification

Professional certifications are another key element of SOC analyst training and career development. Certifications not only validate one's skills and knowledge but are also crucial for career advancement. Some of the most recognized certifications in the field include:

- **CompTIA Security+**: This entry-level certification covers fundamental cybersecurity concepts and practices, serving as a stepping stone for more advanced certifications.

- **Certified Information Systems Security Professional (CISSP)**: A more advanced certification catering to experienced security practitioners, it requires passing a rigorous exam covering various domains of cybersecurity.

- **Certified Ethical Hacker (CEH)**: This certification focuses on penetration testing and ethical hacking skills, allowing analysts to understand how attacks are executed.

- **GIAC Security Essentials Certification (GSEC)**: This certification is designed for professionals who want to demonstrate their knowledge of information security beyond simple terminology and concepts.

- **Certified Incident Handler (GCIH)**: Offered by the GIAC, this certification focuses on incident response and handling skills, ensuring that professionals can effectively respond to and manage security incidents.

19.3 Skills Development and Real-World Application

Skills development is crucial for SOC analysts beyond formal training and certifications. Practical, hands-on experience is invaluable for solidifying knowledge and competencies.

19.3.1 Simulations and Hands-On Labs

Participating in simulations provided by

organizations or training platforms creates realistic scenarios in which SOC analysts can practice their skills. Platforms like Cybersphere, RangeForce, or even custom-built environments can offer labs where analysts can engage in threat detection, incident response, and forensics exercises.

19.3.2 Mentorship Programs

Establishing mentorship programs within organizations can facilitate knowledge sharing and practical guidance. Senior SOC analysts can mentor newer team members, providing insights from their experiences and aiding in their professional growth.

19.3.3 Threat Intelligence Sharing

Collaboration among SOC analysts across sectors can enhance skills and foster a culture of continuous learning. Joining or forming threat intelligence sharing groups enables analysts to share experiences, tactics, and strategies for facing emerging threats.

19.4 Soft Skills Development

While technical expertise is crucial, soft skills are equally important for SOC analysts. Effective communication, problem-solving, and critical thinking skills enhance the analyst's ability to work within a team and respond to security incidents.

19.4.1 Communication Skills

Effective communication is essential, especially during high-pressure incident response situations. SOC analysts must communicate complex technical information clearly and concisely to non-technical stakeholders, ensuring that decisions can be made quickly and accurately.

19.4.2 Teamwork and Collaboration

SOC analysts work closely with IT, legal, and management teams. Fostering teamwork and collaboration skills is essential for functioning well in cross-functional teams during a security incident.

19.4.3 Adaptability and Continuous Learning

The cybersecurity landscape is vibrant and rapidly evolving. SOC analysts must be adaptable and committed to continuous learning to remain relevant and effective. This mindset will enable them to tackle new challenges and threats as they arise.

19.5 The Path Forward: Trends in SOC Analyst Professional Development

Looking forward, SOC analysts must adapt to new trends and technologies shaping the landscape of cybersecurity.

19.5.1 Automation and AI

As automation and artificial intelligence (AI) become more prevalent, SOC analysts will need training that enhances their understanding of these technologies. Familiarity with AI-driven tools that can help detect anomalies and reduce false positives is essential for improving operational efficiency.

19.5.2 Cloud Security

With the increased adoption of cloud technologies, understanding cloud security is imperative. SOC analysts must be trained in protecting cloud environments, including best practices, risk assessments, and incident response specific to cloud infrastructures.

19.5.3 Threat Modeling

To stay ahead of potential threats, SOC analysts should receive training in threat modeling. This proactive approach enables them to identify potential weaknesses in applications or infrastructure and prioritize security measures accordingly.

The journey of a SOC analyst is one of continuous learning and adaptation. As the cybersecurity landscape evolves, so too must the training and professional development of those tasked with securing organizational infrastructures. By focusing on foundational skills, ongoing education, specialization in key areas, and the development of both technical and soft skills, SOC analysts can ensure they remain valuable assets to their organizations in the fight against cyber threats. The investment in training and professional development not only benefits the analysts personally but enhances the overall security posture of organizations, allowing them to face an uncertain future with confidence.

Chapter 20: Best Practices and Guidelines for Security Operations Center (SOC) Analysts

In the realm of cybersecurity, vigilance is key. Security Operations Centers (SOCs) play a critical role in protecting organizations from cyber threats. As threats evolve and become increasingly sophisticated, SOC analysts must adhere to best practices and guidelines to effectively monitor, detect, respond to, and remediate security incidents. This chapter outlines various best practices and guidelines to enhance the efficiency and efficacy of SOC analysts, ensuring that they can maintain robust security postures.

Understanding the SOC Analyst Role

Before delving into best practices, it's essential to delineate the SOC analyst's role within the cybersecurity framework. SOC analysts are responsible for continuously monitoring an organization's IT infrastructure, identifying potential threats, responding to incidents, and coordinating with various stakeholders. Their fundamental responsibilities include:

- **Monitoring security alerts**: Constantly analyzing alerts generated by security tools.

- **Incident analysis**: Investigating security incidents to determine their nature and impact.

- **Response actions**: Taking appropriate actions in response to identified threats.

- **Reporting**: Documenting incidents and producing reports for review.

- **Collaborating**: Working with IT teams, management, and external partners to bolster security measures.

The effectiveness of SOC analysts hinges on a well-defined set of best practices that align with their responsibilities.

1. Continuous Education and Training

Cyber threats are dynamic, meaning that what works today might not be effective tomorrow. Therefore, continuous education and training are paramount for SOC analysts.

- **Regular Workshops**: Organize workshops focusing on emerging threats, vulnerabilities, and new security tools.

- **Certifications**: Encourage analysts to obtain certifications such as Certified Information Systems Security Professional (CISSP), Certified Ethical Hacker (CEH), or CompTIA Security+ to enhance their skills and knowledge.

- **Knowledge Sharing**: Foster a culture of knowledge sharing within the SOC to ensure that analysts are aware of the latest techniques and threats.

2. Utilize a Layered Security Approach

A layered security approach, or defense-in-depth, adds multiple protective measures to protect systems and data. SOC analysts should be familiar with and utilize this strategy, which includes:

- **Firewalls**: Implement and regularly update firewall configurations to filter incoming and outgoing traffic.

- **Intrusion Detection Systems (IDS)**: Deploy IDS to detect and alert on suspicious activity and potential breaches.

- **Endpoint Protection**: Use advanced endpoint detection and response (EDR) solutions to protect devices from malware and other vulnerabilities.

- **Data Encryption**: Ensure that sensitive data is encrypted both in transit and at rest.

3. Effective Security Information and Event Management (SIEM)

A proper SIEM implementation is crucial for any SOC. SIEM solutions aggregate and analyze security data from various sources to identify anomalies and potential threats.

- **Log Management**: Ensure effective log collection, retention, and analysis to facilitate investigations.

- **Correlation Rules**: Develop and fine-tune correlation rules to enhance the accuracy of alerting based on log data.

- **Regular Reviews**: Conduct regular reviews of SIEM configurations and update them as necessary to adapt to new threats.

4. Incident Response Planning

An effective incident response plan (IRP) is crucial for minimizing damage during a security incident.

- **Plan Development**: Develop a comprehensive IRP, defining roles and responsibilities during an incident.

- **Regular Drills**: Conduct simulated incident response exercises to familiarize SOC analysts with procedures and reinforce teamwork.

- **Post-Incident Reviews**: After an incident is resolved, conduct a post-mortem analysis to identify lessons learned and improve response strategies.

5. Prioritize Threat Intelligence

Incorporating threat intelligence into the SOC operations can significantly enhance threat detection and response.

- **Threat Feeds**: Utilize threat intelligence

feeds to stay informed about the latest vulnerabilities, malware, and attack techniques.

- **Use of Threat Models**: Adopt threat modeling frameworks to understand potential threats and prioritize security measures accordingly.

- **Collaboration**: Engage with external threat intelligence sharing communities to gain insights into emerging threats and vulnerabilities.

6. Use Automation Wisely

Automation can significantly enhance the efficiency of SOC operations, but it must be implemented carefully.

- **Automated Alerts**: Utilize automation for alert prioritization to reduce alert fatigue and focus on high-impact incidents.

- **SOAR Solutions**: Implement Security Orchestration, Automation, and Response (SOAR) solutions to streamline incident response processes and minimize response times.

- **Regular Updates and Reviews**: Continuously evaluate automated processes-ensure they remain effective and relevant as threats evolve.

7. Effective Communication and Reporting

Communication plays a critical role in the success of SOC operations.

- **Clear Documentation**: Maintain clear and concise documentation of incidents, processes, and lessons learned to ensure knowledge retention.

- **Management Reporting**: Develop regular reports for management detailing security incidents, response actions, and recommendations to improve security posture.

- **Stakeholder Engagement**: Establish effective channels for communication with stakeholders across the organization, ensuring they are informed of security issues and initiatives.

8. Promote a Security Culture

A strong security culture within the organization can significantly mitigate risks. SOC analysts should contribute to promoting this culture by:

- **User Awareness Programs**: Collaborate with HR and training departments to create and implement security awareness programs for employees.

- **Open Communication**: Encourage a culture where employees feel comfortable reporting suspicious activities.

- **Positive Reinforcement**: Recognize and reward security-minded behavior among employees.

9. Regular Audits and Assessments

Conducting regular audits and assessments can help identify weaknesses within the security posture of the organization.

- **Vulnerability Assessments**: Perform regular scans and assessments to identify potential vulnerabilities and remediate them.

- **Penetration Testing**: Engage in periodic penetration testing to simulate attacks and evaluate the effectiveness of existing security measures.

- **Compliance Audits**: Regularly review compliance with industry frameworks and regulations such as GDPR, HIPAA, or PCI-DSS to maintain legal integrity.

10. Documentation and Knowledge Management

A well-organized documentation and knowledge management approach can serve as a valuable resource for SOC analysts.

- **Knowledge Base**: Create a centralized knowledge base where analysts can access incident reports, playbooks, and threat intelligence.

- **WIKI or Intranet**: Maintain an internal WIKI or intranet site where SOC guidelines, processes, and best practices are easily accessible.

- **Incident Log Management**: Maintain a clear record of past incidents, responses, and outcomes to aid future investigations.

Conclusion

The landscape of cybersecurity is constantly changing, and SOC analysts must adapt to meet new challenges. By following these best practices and guidelines, SOC analysts can enhance their effectiveness and contribute to a more secure organizational environment. Continuous education, robust communication, effective use of technology, and a proactive posture toward threats will empower SOC analysts to safeguard their organizations effectively.

The commitment to ongoing improvement and adaptation to emerging threats will ensure that the SOC remains a key player in the overall cybersecurity strategy. Ultimately, the effectiveness of a SOC is directly influenced by the skill, knowledge, and practices of its analysts, making their continuous growth and maturity essential for lasting success in the ever-evolving domain of cybersecurity.

Glossary

Glossary of Technical Terms for SOC Analysts (Levels 1, 2, 3, and 4)

Introduction

In the ever-evolving landscape of cybersecurity, Security Operations Center (SOC) Analysts play a crucial role in protecting organizations from cyber threats. The following glossary aims to provide clarity on the terminology and concepts that SOC Analysts—across different levels—encounter in their daily operations. This detailed glossary is structured to facilitate understanding for SOC Analysts at levels 1-4.

Level 1 SOC Analyst Terms

1. **Alert**: A notification generated by security tools when suspicious activity is detected. Alerts can vary in severity and may require further investigation.

2. **Incident**: A confirmed occurrence of a security event that has compromised the confidentiality, integrity, or availability of an information asset.

3. **Phishing**: A cyber attack that attempts to trick individuals into providing sensitive information by masquerading as a trustworthy entity in electronic communications.

4. **Malware**: Malicious software designed to cause harm, exploit, or otherwise compromise a system or network. Types include viruses, worms, Trojans, ransomware, and spyware.

5. **Log**: A recorded piece of data

generated by devices and applications that can be used for monitoring, troubleshooting, or forensic analysis.

6. **Firewall**: A security system that monitors and controls incoming and outgoing network traffic based on predetermined security rules.

7. **SIEM (Security Information and Event Management)**: A security solution that collects, analyzes, and correlates security data from across the organization in real-time for better incident response.

8. **Endpoint**: Any device that connects to a network, such as computers, servers, and mobile devices. Endpoint security involves protecting these devices from cyber threats.

9. **Vulnerability**: A weakness in a system, application, or network that can potentially be

exploited by attackers.

10. **Threat**: Any potential danger that could exploit a vulnerability and cause harm to an organization's information or systems.

Level 2 SOC Analyst Terms

11. **Threat Intelligence**: Data that has been analyzed to provide insights into existing and emerging threats that could potentially impact an organization.

12. **Incident Response Plan**: A documented strategy outlining how an organization will respond to cybersecurity incidents, including identification, containment, eradication, and recovery.

13. **Forensics**: The practice of collecting, preserving, and analyzing digital evidence to understand the details of a cyber incident and identify the perpetrators.

14. **Malware Analysis**: The process of analyzing malicious software to understand its behavior, functionality, and potential impact on systems.

15. **Intrusion Detection System (IDS)**: A security tool that monitors network traffic for suspicious activity and alerts administrators when potentially malicious behavior is detected.

16. **Intrusion Prevention System (IPS)**: Similar to IDS, but with the added functionality of actively blocking or mitigating malicious traffic.

17. **Threat Hunting**: Proactive search for threats within a network, beyond established alerts, often using threat intelligence and behavioral analysis.

18. **Patch Management**: The process of applying updates to software and systems to fix vulnerabilities and improve security.

19. **Access Control**: A security technique that limits access to systems or information to authorized users. This can include authentication methods and user permissions.

20. **Social Engineering**: Manipulative techniques used by attackers to trick individuals into divulging confidential information or performing actions that compromise security.

Level 3 SOC Analyst Terms

21. **Advanced Persistent Threat (APT)**: A prolonged and targeted cyber attack wherein an intruder gains access to a network and remains undetected for an extended period.

22. **Zero-Day Exploit**: A vulnerability in software that is unknown to the vendor and has no available fix or patch at the time of discovery by hackers.

23. **Denial of Service (DoS)**: An attack aimed at making a network or service unavailable by overwhelming it with traffic or requests.

24. **Data Exfiltration**: The unauthorized transfer of data from a computer or network, typically carried out by cybercriminals after a

successful breach.

25. **Network Traffic Analysis**: The examination of data flows within a network to identify patterns and detect potential security incidents.

26. **Sandboxing**: An isolation technique that allows the testing of untrusted programs in a controlled environment where they cannot harm other systems.

27. **Encryption**: The process of converting data into a coded format to prevent unauthorized access. Decryption is the process of converting it back to its original format.

28. **Public Key Infrastructure (PKI)**: A framework that enables secure communications through the use of public-key cryptography, which includes digital certificates and certificate authorities.

29. **Compliance**: Adherence to laws, regulations, and standards that govern data protection and security practices, such as GDPR, HIPAA, and PCI DSS.

30. **Incident Reporting**: The formal documentation of details regarding a security incident, which is vital for analysis, improving future responses, and fulfilling compliance requirements.

Level 4 SOC Analyst Terms

31. **Incident Management**: The holistic approach for managing the lifecycle of incidents, including identification, categorization, prioritization, response, and closure.

32. **Root Cause Analysis (RCA)**: A method of problem-solving used to identify the underlying reasons for faults or problems in order to prevent recurrence.

33. **Behavioral Analytics**: The use of machine learning to analyze behavioral patterns in order to identify anomalies that may indicate a security issue.

34. **Red Team/Blue Team Exercises**: Security exercises where a red team simulates an attack (offensive) while the blue team defends against it (defensive) to improve security posture.

35. **Security Posture**: The overall cybersecurity strength and readiness of an organization, including its capabilities and the measures implemented to prevent and respond to threats.

36. **Risk Assessment**: A process of identifying and analyzing potential risks that could negatively impact an organization's assets or operations.

37. **Business Continuity Plan (BCP)**: A strategy that outlines how an organization will continue operating during and after a significant disruption or incident.

38. **Disaster Recovery Plan (DRP)**: A documented process or set of procedures to recover and protect a business IT infrastructure in the event of a disaster.

39. **Supply Chain Security**: Practices aimed at protecting the organization's supply chain from cybersecurity risks throughout the lifecycle of products and services.

40. **Security Operations**: The day-to-day activities and processes carried out by a SOC to monitor, detect, respond to, and mitigate cybersecurity threats.

Index

339